Praise for *Every Gift Matters*

"Carrie Morgridge has written a must-read primer for anyone considering philanthropy. From the smallest gifts to transformative mega-giving, she shows her readers how passion, smarts, and trust can change the world. Read this book and learn from one of the best."

—**Katherine Bradley, President, CityBridge Foundation**

"*In Every Gift Matters*, Morgridge reminds us that we are a nation of "difference makers" and encourages us to continue that legacy of meaningful giving through her empowering stories of those who have made a difference."

—**Douglas Conant, Chairman, Avon Products; Chairman, Kellogg Executive Leadership Institute; Founder & CEO, ConantLeadership; Former CEO & President, Campbell Soup Company**

"*Every Gift Matters* is a collection of timely, personal stories reminding us that philanthropy isn't about writing a check; it's about the value we create when we invest in local communities, follow our principles, and make a lasting difference."

—**Howard W. Buffet, Lecturer in International and Public Affairs, Columbia University**

"*Every Gift Matters* inspires readers to reimagine the transformative nature of giving. Through engaging stories and real-world examples, Carrie provides a new roadmap to more meaningful and impactful philanthropy."

—**Bill Goodwyn, CEO, Discovery Education**

"Carrie Morgridge shows firsthand how philanthropy multiplies the happiness and wellbeing of both giver and receiver, well beyond all material benefits. She is among the most vivacious and successful philanthropists I have had the pleasure of knowing, and her book is a challenge to the rest of us to step up our game."

—**Arthur C. Brooks, President, American Enterprise Institute**

"Carrie Morgridge is among the most hands-on, proactive philanthropists I've ever encountered. *Every Gift Matters* reflects how thoughtfulness and passion can multiply one's impact in philanthropy."

—**Hadi Patrovi, Founder, Code.org**

"Anyone interested in philanthropy can learn from *Every Gift Matters*. It's a must-read if you want to learn how to effectively support the causes you believe in and feel that your dollars are actually making a difference."

—**Jeffrey C. Walker, Author, *The Generosity Network***

"Carrie Morgridge is an amazing force of nature who is reshaping the world by improving the lives of countless thousands by her passionate, kind-hearted love. Carrie's generosity, organizational excellence, and infectious enthusiasm know no bounds. In *Every Gift Matters*, you will not only be inspired by acts of selfless compassion and joy, but Carrie shows how even the most modest acts of philanthropy can have a most meaningful impact upon the lives of others."

—**Mark Holtzman, Chairman, Meridian Capital HK**

"This is a must-read for anyone who wants to make a difference. As one of the savviest philanthropists I know, Carrie Morgridge knows how to make the most of her giving. *Every Gift Matters* shows that transformative giving is about much more than the number of zeros on your check."

—**Mark Tercek, CEO, The Nature Conservancy**

"For anyone with the passion and caring to do more, *Every Gift Matters* will become your go-to guide for giving."

—**Dr. Pamela Cantor, Founder, Turnaround for Children Inc.**

"Carrie Morgridge and The Morgridge Family Foundation are truly gifts to Colorado. In *Every Gift Matters*, Carrie reminds us that we can impact positive and extraordinary change in the communities where we live, in such a compelling way!"

—**Gov. John Hickenlooper, Governor of Colorado**

"In *Every Gift Matters*, Carrie Morgridge transforms the way we look at giving, teaching us that you can't remove the donor from their donation. She shows us how the best giving works as a circle, feeding itself and growing in impact, not just a one-way, one-time transfer of resources, and she speaks with the authority and wisdom of someone who is making these things happen in her own life everyday!"

—Stacey Stewart, US President, United Way Worldwide

Every
Gift
Matters

How Your Passion Can Change the World

CARRIE
MORGRIDGE

with John Perry

GREENLEAF
BOOK GROUP PRESS

Published by Greenleaf Book Group Press
Austin, Texas
www.gbgpress.com

Distributed by Greenleaf Book Group

For ordering information or special discounts for bulk purchases, please contact
Greenleaf Book Group at PO Box 91869, Austin, TX 78709, 512.891.6100.

Design and composition by Greenleaf Book Group and Kim Lance
Cover design by Greenleaf Book Group and Kim Lance
Cover image: Thinkstock/iStock Collection/boule13

Cataloging-in-Publication data is available

ISBN: 978-1-62634-182-1
eBook ISBN: 978-1-62634-183-8

Part of the Tree Neutral® program, which offsets the number of trees
consumed in the production and printing of this book by taking proactive
steps, such as planting trees in direct proportion to the number of trees
used: www.treeneutral.com

TreeNeutral®

Printed in the United States of America on acid-free paper

15 16 17 18 19 20   10 9 8 7 6 5 4 3 2 1

First Edition

To my husband John, who has loved me unconditionally since the first day we met. You are my rock solid, and I love you with all my heart.

To my two children John and Michelle: John you are so smart, sometimes I don't understand how you have that much knowledge up in your head. Like your dad, you both are amazing with the facts and data. Michelle, you are turning into your mother, which is a compliment! As the reader gets to know me in this book, they will also get to know you. You are beautiful on the inside as well as on the outside.

To John and Tashia Morgridge, thank you for believing in me and loving me right from the beginning. Thank you for always encouraging me to do more, learn more, strive for greatness and allowing me to make mistakes.

To my parents and stepparents, Val and Ken and Terry and Alex. I feel so lucky to have two full sets of parents, who love me, give me advice, challenge me and believe that I have unlimited potential.

To Mark Hayes and Geof Rochester, for three years you both begged me to write a book and share my private stories about giving and dot connecting. Mark, thank you for introducing me to Robert.

To Robert and Bobbie Wolgemuth, my agents! I have been so blessed to work with you both this past year. Thank you for the support, the prayers when I needed them and the encouragement to continue. Thank you for allowing me into your personal prayer circle. God Bless.

To my writer John Perry, thank you for spending countless hours on the phone and email with me. You have taught me so much. Thank you for coming to the KIPP event with me in Chicago to meet Malcolm Gladwell! Nothing will ever replace face-to-face meetings.

To John Farnam and Paul Heitzenrater, thank you for the encouragement, guidance, laughs, and late night garden parties. You have taught me the power of taking care of your own backyard.

To Dr. Michael Salem, *so much to be grateful for, mostly your friendship which I treasure.*

To Donna Di Ianni, Denise Roberts and Stefanie Borsari, *thank you for running all the behind the scenes back office. You make the foundation the best it can be, and we thank you.*

To Elliott Robinson, *thank you for changing my life forever. You introduced me to Ironman and I am forever grateful.*

To Sarah Dunn and Kim Sasko, *thank you for working so hard for teachers with the expansion of Share Fair Nation. It takes a team, and you are the best.*

To Red and Black, *it is amazing what one pair of shoes can do. Thank you for the introduction to Greenleaf Book Group. You were right; they are great! Thank you for teaching me the importance of real paper books.*

To Dr. Jamie Van Leeuwen, *I saw in you what so many see in me, unlimited potential. Thank you for all the collaborations, and teaching me all about homelessness. I am forever changed. Let Po.*

To Christine Benero, *thank you for always leading with your heart! Your compassion and brilliant leadership have shaped our world.*

To all the nonprofits, foundations and volunteers we have met, and to those of you we have not met—*Thank You! Thank you for what you do each and every day. Thank you for never giving up when things get hard. Thank you for teaching people like me. Thank you for all the good you do and all the amazing people you rally to become Difference Makers!*

If you want to touch the past,
touch a rock.

If you want to touch the present,
touch a flower.

If you want to touch the future,
touch a life.

—Author unknown

Contents

Foreword

There are numerous books and articles on the do's and don'ts of giving that explain how to be a more impactful philanthropist. So what makes this book different? *Every Gift Matters: How Your Passion Can Change the World* teaches not with facts and figures but with the stories behind them: first-person examples of the "how to" of joyful giving. It will teach and inspire you and, I hope, trigger your own giving passion. Giving is a multi-faceted opportunity of time, knowledge, and dollars. This book speaks to each.

Our son, John, and his wife, Carrie, set up the Morgridge Family Foundation about fifteen years ago, funded by an annual grant from the TOSA Foundation established by my wife, Tashia, and me. Ever since, John and Carrie have worked diligently at becoming more effective philanthropists. As you will see from the stories Carrie shares here, they have continuously evolved their methods and approach. As a result, they have also modified their focus, learning from experience as they go. One of the keys to their model is the art of working with and through others, capitalizing on the leverage that teamwork provides. A caution: this model also demands a high level of personal involvement. As their stories so vividly demonstrate, personal involvement and collaboration with others are foundational elements of their success.

Your journey will be different. Yet whatever your passion and however much you have to give, you can use the techniques on display here and follow the numerous signposts Carrie has set out. While not guaranteed, these guides should help you find fulfillment, joy, and perhaps fun in your successful philanthropic activities.

Throughout its history, our country has provided many opportunities for individuals to accumulate significant wealth. Uniquely, at the same time our people have a DNA for unusual generosity. "In 2013, the largest source of charitable giving came from individuals at $241.32 billion."[1]

Two successful start-ups provided the wherewithal for my wife and me to become major donors. However, the need and personal desire to "pay it forward" was always a part of us, as reflected in our $15 donation to our alma mater over fifty years ago. Though since then our ability to give has grown, our joy in giving wisely remains one of the constants in our lives.

For over thirty years, giving of our time, knowledge, and dollars has enriched our lives and given us great joy.

—*John P. Morgridge*
Chairman Emeritus, Cisco Systems

Preface

e write a book? It had never entered my mind. Yes, I knew plenty of stories about incredible people who dedicated themselves to helping others. Yes, I'd learned a lot about giving—and how not to give. I had worked with inspiring friends like Kellie Lauth, Dave Krepcho, Mandy Williams, young Kylan, and many others. But I didn't have the time to write a book about them.

At least that's what I said the day I got a call while riding mountain bikes with my husband, John. It was my friend Mark Hayes telling me about a couple he and his wife had met at church, Robert and Bobbie Wolgemuth. Robert was a literary agent and Mark had shared a little of my story with him. Robert and I got acquainted by phone on the spot. We talked until I was getting so winded by the ride that I actually had to pull over to continue the conversation.

As I will mention in Chapter 1, Mark had been after me for a while to write a book. And he had another wonderful friend named Geof Rochester. These guys were relentless. Every time I saw either of them they would ask, "When are you going to write a book?" Connecting with Robert made me think that maybe I could pull it off after all.

I had developed a new appreciation for the power of books. Some of them became the backbone for business and emotional decisions that forever shaped me. First of all, I had become addicted to mysteries from writers such as Patricia Cornwell, Dan Brown, Anne Perry, James Patterson, and more—they proved how exciting and memorable books can be. Also, I realized how much I could learn from visionary business writers. One day, while visiting my father-in-law at Stanford, I was in the business section of the library and discovered Jim Collins. His books *Good to Great: Why Some Companies Make the Leap . . . And Others Don't* (New York: HarperBusiness, 2001) and *Built to Last: Successful Habits of Visionary Companies* (New York: HarperBusiness, 1994) transformed my thinking about leadership. From there I went to Malcolm Gladwell, whose *Outliers: The Story of Success* (New York: Little, Brown, 2008) gave me the permission I needed to run our foundation differently and look for new perspectives. In that moment, I determined that there was power in the printed word. I realized that I could share my stories and make a case for smart philanthropy.

To help with the nuts and bolts of the process, Robert recommended a writer client of his named John Perry. After speaking with John once on the phone, I knew he was the person I wanted to work with. By then I already had the beginning of what I thought would be a good book—with a working title of *The Dot Connector*. As a philanthropist, that's how I saw myself, and how my connections in the philanthropic community saw me. We all soon agreed that the only problem with the idea was that it was really boring. We kept looking for a more exciting way to tell the story.

One day I was on the phone with John Perry telling him about Student Support Foundation clubs and how $100 invested in the correct way could literally change somebody's life. There was story after story of the thoughtful grants the students had awarded to deserving recipients. Though our foundation sponsored the clubs, the kids made all the funding decisions themselves. I believed in them, and that gave them the courage to take responsibility for how the money was spent. They learned that even a small amount, when invested wisely, could pay big dividends—both in the result achieved and in the great satisfaction the giver was able to experience.

Bingo! This is the book!

That realization put us on the right track. From there, we wrote the first three chapters and were on our way.

At first I felt my way along very carefully. This was unfamiliar territory. I can speak in front of an audience all day. I can run a meeting anywhere. But writing is another matter. In the beginning, I wouldn't let anyone else see the manuscript. Only John Perry and I saw it as it was being written. But as the book grew more mature, I adopted the process I always prefer: putting together a team to work with me. A group of articulate, reliable friends with different viewpoints is a great way to get the most out of an idea.

From Robert and writer-John, I enlarged the circle to include husband-John (always my best and most encouraging critic, who gave up countless mountain bike rides while I sat writing), and three wise and trusted friends to lend fresh eyes to the project. John Farnam remembered so many stories in the book because he was there for most of them. Kim Sasko is new to our team. Nonetheless, her editorial observations were always spot on, and she was instrumental in making the emotional link in our stories.

Sarah Dunn helped especially with the flow of the stories and with the cohesiveness of content throughout the chapters. She also caught mistakes (like when I mixed up Malcolm Gladwell's books *Outliers* and *Blink*). All these efforts allowed for a much more enjoyable read, trust me. In the end, it was John Perry who listened to me for so long then thoughtfully reassembled the pieces, embedding some wonderful color into these true stories.

Until I started this writing adventure, I had never looked back at our grants or their recipients. I'm always looking ahead instead—it's just the way I'm wired. Looking back was always a challenging and emotional journey. Revisiting the stories of so many dedicated people has been a humbling reminder of the incredible good that people around the country do every day. While I was able to help them, they were helping me by teaching me to look at the joy of giving in a whole new light.

Your time, your money, your passion, and your caring will keep the circle going. You might never meet any of the people you choose to help, but every one of them is a starfish tossed back into the sea with a new life in front of them.

For all you've done and for all you will do, thank you.

Chapter 1

The $7 Miracle

A boy walked along the shore at low tide. With each step, his small feet left a perfect imprint behind in the sand. A line of seaweed, shells, and sea foam marked where the water had lapped up onto the beach, depositing whatever it carried there along the margin between land and sea.

As the cool waves rushed in over his toes, the boy looked down and saw a starfish half-buried in the sand. It had been washed ashore and was now stranded, baking helplessly in the morning sun. Looking ahead along the beach he saw dozens, maybe hundreds, of other starfish in the same predicament.

He bent down and picked up a starfish, throwing it as hard and as far as he could back into the life-giving water. Reaching down for the next starfish, he threw it back, too. Then another, and then another.

The boy's mother, walking some distance behind him, called out his name. He turned to look. "Why are you working so hard?" she gently scolded, her voice lifted loud enough to be heard above the surf. "There are too many starfish. What you're doing doesn't matter."

And of course it was true. For every one he could rescue, many more would perish in the scorching heat.

Yet he picked up another starfish and held it high for her to see.

"It matters to this one," he said determinedly, and heaved it as far as he could into the ocean.

The boy couldn't save every starfish. But he could save the one in his hand and as many as he could toss back into the water.

This is a wonderful picture of philanthropy. Each person and every gift can make a difference. Whoever you are, no matter how much or how little you have, your gift matters. The smallest, seemingly unimportant, donation can transform a life. And the best news is that giving transforms two lives: the one who receives and the one who gives. Some would even say that the giver receives much more than the recipient

This is a book about giving. About celebrating the joy of doing what you can for people who are truly in need. It's a book filled with stories and experiences that my husband, John, and I have shared about making gifts both large and small: how to turn your gifts into investments that grow over time, compounding the gift to others. How to leverage a gift of either time or money, regardless of size, to make it work harder, work smarter, and have a bigger impact on your community. How the gift of time can be one of the greatest gifts of all—volunteers are some of the most successful and respected philanthropists I know.

You'll discover that the effect of your generosity on others isn't the best part. The best part about giving is the irrepressible happiness that comes from having a generous heart—the enjoyment and fulfillment that giving can bring. Showing compassion for others is a great way to reenergize your own spirit. It's a natural high I never get tired of experiencing.

One of the most important lessons I've learned is that life-changing gifts can be small. Most of the money donated to nonprofits in America comes from households that give a total of $2,000 a year, on average. Even though John and I give large gifts through our family foundation, I've seen a $7 gift change a child's life forever. Every dollar truly can make a difference. I'll prove to you from my own experience that this is true.

I must admit that writing about philanthropy (or anything else, for that matter) takes me out of my comfort zone. I'm doing it because two wonderful friends would not take "No" for an answer. The first was Mark Hayes, a successful investor and entrepreneur who is also the education program director at Lake Nona Institute, near Orlando. This is part of a huge community centered around Florida's Medical City—where there are plans to build fifteen new schools. The developer there invited me to be their educational advisor for pre-K–12. I jumped at the chance because foundations rarely get a chance to partner with new schools. We generally go in after a school is already failing and hope for the best. It was Mark who first said to me, "You can't keep all this knowledge in education bottled up. You need to write a book!"

My second cheerleader was Geof Rochester, managing director at The Nature Conservancy, one of the most important conservation organizations in the world. Together we launched an interactive website for kids called Nature Works Everywhere (www.natureworkseverywhere.org), a fun, hands-on learning site used by more than three million children. Geof told me I should write a book in order to share what I'd learned about giving by rolling up my sleeves and getting involved. I've made some successful grants and some unsuccessful ones, and learned a lot from each. Every time I saw Geof, he would needle me in a friendly way, "When is your book coming out?" I can scarcely wait for the day I put a copy of this in his hand.

Any conversation about giving eventually comes around to money. The money itself isn't the solution. It's a tool. In the right hands, in the right situation, it can literally work miracles. And, like any tool, you have to know how to use it to get the most out of it. Side by side with the conversation about money, the discussion has to include how to make a program sustainable, how to attract volunteers, and how to leverage the gift to fully maximize its value.

There are millions of people out there that need your support, just like the starfish on the shore. Sometimes it is a hand up; sometimes it is a restart on life. They may need a fresh start, a second chance, or temporary help getting over a rough spot. Life leaves us all stranded at one time or another. We shouldn't be ashamed to ask for help when we need it, and we shouldn't hesitate to offer help when we can give it. No one person or organization can identify every need or fill every gap. This is why an ongoing spirit of giving is so important for you to nurture.

The more you know about how to give effectively, the bigger impact your gift will make—regardless of size—and the more joy and satisfaction it will bring you in return.

We are a nation of givers. In good economic times and bad, Americans give about 2 percent of the gross domestic product in contributions to nonprofits, churches, and other causes.[2] It can be intimidating to hear about foundations making very large donations. Those big numbers can reinforce the notion that small individual donations don't matter. Well here's a surprise. For every dollar American foundations give each year, individual donors give $5. In other words, all together, individual American households donate five times as much to charities and other nonprofits as all the foundations in the country combined. According to figures published by the National Philanthropic Trust, the total of charitable contributions from American households in 2013 added up to more than $241 *billion*.[3] That's a lot of happy givers.

I don't have all the answers when it comes to giving money, but I have a lot more experience than the average person. Over the past fifteen years I have volunteered more than ten thousand hours of my time with organizations I feel passionate about. As Malcolm Gladwell explained in chapter 2 of his book *Outliers*, at ten thousand hours you become an expert at whatever you've invested the time in. I still have plenty to learn about giving, but I've gotten really good at identifying a great program from a not-so-great program. In all those hours there are many experiences that illustrate key lessons that I've discovered about smart philanthropy. I'll be introducing you to some awesome people and organizations that taught me so much and that mean so much to me as a donor.

My hours of volunteering have reinforced the crucial point that every gift matters. The idea that "my gift is too small to make any difference" is a self-defeating notion. It's time to blow up that idea for good!

Remember earlier I shared with you that $7 could change a life? One example of how a small gift can make a huge difference is a program called Book Trust. This is a nonprofit organization that inspires kids' passion for reading by empowering children from low-income families to choose books that they will own. Students get a $7 allowance per month to order books from the Scholastic Reading Club, which will buy two or three books of their choice.

Access to books is a leading predictor of a child's success in school. The average middle-income child has thirteen books at home, while in low-income communities there's an average of one book for every three hundred children![4] According to the Annie E. Casey Foundation, which has supported disadvantaged children around the country for more than sixty years, a child who can't read by the third grade is four times more likely to drop out of school than a child who can read at grade level.[5]

Amy Friedman, executive director of Book Trust (www .booktrust.org), explains, "The more literate people we have in our community, the more likely we're going to have a highly productive and successful community . . . Literacy is the civil rights challenge of our generation, and we have an obligation to ensure the success of our kids."

As with every giving decision, there were plenty of options to consider. Why did we select Book Trust when there are hundreds of nonprofits in the same category out there competing for funds? The first reason was that Book Trust does so much with so little. Seven dollars a month can work miracles in a young student's life. The second reason was that Book Trust was a local charity started by a family in Colorado, where we live. I like investing in an organization that is part of my community. It makes for easy access, freely sharing ideas, and getting to know the founders and staff. Several other characteristics spun off from those two reasons. They're things I always look for when I consider making a gift:

- **An atmosphere of trust and understanding:** For us, the most successful philanthropic relationships are the ones built on respect, personal friendships, and mutual trust. Book Trust was founded by the Schatz family in Fort Collins after their daughter, Adrienne, noticed that not all the kids in her class were ordering from the Scholastic Reading Club each month. As we got to know the family, we began to feel these connections, and our funding grew with our trust level. Since the operation was local, we got to spend a ton of time with the staff as well, sharing our ideas on growth.

- **Shared goals and values:** The Morgridge Family Foundation and Book Trust shared the same goals for giving—to impact as many students as possible by providing access to books of their very own. We saw the potential for Book Trust to expand on a national scale. As Jim Collins, author of *Good to Great*, would put it, the flywheel was already there to create a partnership between Book Trust and Scholastic. We wanted to accelerate their national expansion.

- **Immediate impact:** As soon as we approved an initial grant, Book Trust put it to work to buy books for children that same month. The process and bureaucracy were minimal; the benefit came right away.

- **Leverage:** For every Scholastic book children ordered through Book Trust, the teachers earned Scholastic Bonus Points, which they could use to get more free books and classroom supplies. This multiplied the buying power of every dollar we gave.

- **Ripple effect:** I love it when a donation has additional benefits I never expected. In this case, the free books encouraged learning not only in the classroom but also at home, where children read to their siblings. Some—especially kids from families that don't speak English at home—even read to their parents. Book Trust classrooms saw a nearly

30 percent increase in the number of students reading at grade level by the end of the 2013–2014 school year.

- **Small gifts, big result:** Though Book Trust has big goals, an important chunk of their support comes from very modest gifts. Scholastic Reading Club members anywhere in the country can donate to Book Trust by adding as little as $1 to their order forms. During the second half of the 2012–2013 school year, these $1 gifts totaled more than $150,000, enough to supply more than two thousand kids with new books for the school year. As a result, those kids are *four times more likely* to finish high school because they will develop the reading skills they need.

- **Compounded giving:** Over time, modest gifts wisely invested can grow in an amazing way. When a nonprofit is smart about spending they're likely to attract larger gifts. We started with an entry-level contribution to Book Trust. Once we saw the result, we gave more. Our ability to give is always limited by our annual budget, but over time our gifts compounded so that the total impact has been very rewarding to them, and a joy for us. Since 2007, the Morgridge Family Foundation cumulative investment in Book Trust provided for nearly 600,000 new books for almost 27,000 low-income students. On top of that, these young readers' teachers have earned more than eight million Scholastic Bonus Points to buy more books, supplies, and even iPads for their classrooms.

But the kids don't care about any of that. They care about the day the books arrive. As they crowd around excitedly, their teacher opens the big box and starts handing out its treasures. Eager hands reach out as each name is called. Finally all the boys and girls hold books that they picked out themselves, spontaneously breaking into circles and reading to each other. Excited shouts and beaming smiles fill the classroom. Teachers tell us that they now carve out time just for the students to read and share together—filled with the thrill of discovery and adventure the new books bring.

Adams 12 Five Star School District Superintendent Chris Gdowski reads this first grader one of his Book Trust books.

Wherever I find organizations to support, whatever amount I decide to give, it all comes down to partnering with people who share my passion and my conviction that every dollar can always work harder. This is my life—a small-town California girl with big dreams who is grateful every day for the path her life has taken and the chance to give back.

Chapter 2

A Grateful Life

My day starts early. I'm up at 5:00 to feed the hummingbirds and take the dog out. My first conference call is usually around 7:15. There's a stack of mail on the table. I dig into it with joy because there are always thank-you notes from students and teachers across the United States expressing their thanks and appreciation for bringing technology into their classrooms—iPads, interactive whiteboards, connections with online learning sites, and other exciting new educational tools. Today's comments from a fourth grade class include

"The new iPads are fun to use even though I don't like math."

"We are setting up a cool new lab. Thank you so much!"

"You are very kind for helping us."

"Thank you for this great gift, and may the galaxy be kind to you."

It's a busy world filled with decisions about where to focus my time and resources, but I love every minute of it. Nothing gives me more satisfaction than to share what I have with others.

Yet it wasn't always this way. The life I have today is a long way from where I started.

I'm actually a very ordinary person. I didn't start out with any special insights or wisdom. What I did have from the beginning was a love of learning and a willingness to work. I still like to work hard and play hard. I love to celebrate successes and learn from my mistakes. I get excited when I see something making a positive difference in someone else's life. One of my greatest pleasures is knowing that people who are doing the best they can and want to do better are getting the support and encouragement they need.

The world I see doesn't have a lot of gray in it. I either love something or I don't. I love learning, teaching, music, the outdoors, sports, dogs, good writers, good thinkers, good red wine, change, and the word YES. There's no place in my world for phony people, big talkers who don't deliver, crappy administrators, or whiners.

I believe my heart for education came from my parents. One of my earliest memories is of them reading to me at night before bed. I loved the sound of my mother's voice. She would always tell me I could be anything I wanted to be. I could do anything I set my heart to. Her encouragement has stayed with me to this day.

Mom and Dad had met and married after Dad got back from the Naval Hospital located in Guam during the Vietnam Conflict in August 1964. When I came along, Mom babysat other children at home so she could be with me, while Dad went to college full-time and held down two jobs at night. We lived in a modest two-bedroom house in Santa Barbara near the freeway. As tight as things were, they were determined to give me the best education they could. Instead of going to the neighborhood public school, I went to the private Christian school downtown.

I'll never forget my kindergarten teacher, Mrs. Hall. She had bright red hair tucked up like Lucille Ball. She seemed very tall and skinny to me and always wore colored hose, which is what we kindergarteners saw at eye level most of the time. I remember how she used to hug us and praise us for our work.

Financially, things must not have been going so great after a couple of years, because by second grade my parents decided it was time for me to go to public school. Though I was only in second grade, I tested at a fifth-grade level. The principal asked my parents if I could skip a couple grades, but they both felt this would be hard on me because my social skills hadn't developed enough. That was fine with me. I remember a wonderful year of walking to school, joining the Girl Scouts, and just being a kid.

Third grade was a very different story. That year I went back to the private school downtown and was a complete failure. Going to the public school for second grade was like missing an entire year of learning. I was getting Fs on all my papers. I was so worried about school that I wasn't even paying attention to the fact that my parents' marriage was coming apart. Right before winter break they sat me down to tell me they were divorcing and I was moving in with my mother and her parents. Mom and Dad loved me with all their hearts, but they couldn't stay together. To be honest, I was happy. I loved my grandparents. I spent every Saturday night at their house watching Lawrence Welk and playing Chinese checkers with my grandma. We went to church on Sunday mornings where I got to learn fascinating stories from the Bible, play outside with all the kids, and listen to my grandpa proudly sing in the choir. How great would it be living with them full time? What I didn't know or understand was my new world meant being apart from my dad.

Mom then moved to San Luis Obispo and remarried, so I had

to change schools for fourth grade. Luckily it was another private school. The only pitfall was riding the bus an hour each way every day. The next year we moved to a small town up the coast, so I switched schools again. I ended up going to five different elementary schools in six years.

Middle and high school seemed to fly by. My middle school teacher said I had a great talent for math and encouraged me to stick with it. I got an A in algebra, which allowed me to go all the way through high school with only one more year of math. (It seems ironic to me that even then teachers rewarded the best math students with fewer math requirements, instead of encouraging them to tackle more advanced courses.)

While things at school were mostly good, things at home were not so hot. I didn't like my stepfather very much. In December of my senior year I turned eighteen and, being fed up with my living situation, I moved out. I had a great job as a grocery store checker. For somebody my age, the pay was amazing. The first place I lived in on my own was a refinished garage. It was small, but I was free from the intense living situation! My roommate and I split the $100 monthly rent, my dad bought me an old reliable car, and I was ready to take on the world!

I picked up every shift I could at the grocery store. As members of a union, the checkers got pay increases based on time worked, and I was racking up the shifts. Soon my roommate and another girl and I were able to move into a real apartment. Actually it was a dump, but it had three bedrooms, three baths, and a full-sized kitchen. Since I was a high school senior and my roommates were over twenty-one, I had a lot of fun the second half of the school year. Word gets around pretty quickly when you're on your own and you have the party house. I found myself popular for the first time. Everyone enjoyed coming over and hanging out.

Even though I'd done well in school in the past, I barely graduated. I had enough credits, but I needed to pass this one political science class with Mr. Burns. Part of the reason I was failing was that I never turned in the homework. To do the assignments I had to look up current events in the newspaper, but I couldn't afford to buy one. Mr. Burns called me into his office and told me if I didn't get help, I was going to fail his class and wouldn't be able to graduate. I broke down and shared my situation with him. He offered to help me with a tutor—my friend Alice. I would meet with Alice once a week at the pizza parlor next to the grocery store where I worked.

I was always amazed that Mr. Burns was having pizza with his family every time I was being tutored. It wasn't until much later that I realized how much he really cared about me, and how badly he wanted me to succeed. He was following up to make sure I got the help I needed. I passed his class by one point. Actually, there were so many kids failing that he graded on a huge curve, so I passed with room to spare.

After graduation I had my heart set on getting out of the small town where I lived, just up the coast from San Luis Obispo. I moved to San Francisco and got married. By the time I was twenty-one, I was divorced and on my own again. Silicon Valley was just starting to take off in the Bay Area, and if you wanted to work hard and get ahead, San Francisco was the place to be. I got a job with a real estate agency and soon loved life again. The real estate market was booming in the 1980s and continues to boom today thanks to the inventors, creators, and entrepreneurs all around the Valley.

But on October 17, 1989, my world was shaken—literally—by the Loma Prieta earthquake. At 6.9 on the Richter scale, it was one of the most powerful in California history, injuring thousands and leaving thousands more homeless. Because it happened during warm-up practice for the World Series between the Oakland Athletics and the San Francisco Giants, it was the first major earthquake to be broadcast live on national television. As I watched the marina in flames, I decided I needed to move out of the city. The next morning I packed my car and drove to Alameda, a town on an island in the eastern part of San Francisco Bay.

Coming to a new neighborhood and making new friends, I found myself playing a ton of beach volleyball on weekends. Sports always brought out the best in me. That's where I met a couple who owned a tanning salon. They let me trade out working there for tanning time. I really thought their business was cool. The customers all seemed happy and had fun, the business made good money, and I could see myself owning a tanning salon and becoming my own boss. This was the business for me! My next step was to write a business plan and start working a second job to save for a down payment.

Dad had become a successful accountant, so I spent every weekend I could with him in Fresno working on my plan. True to character, he made sure our time together wasn't all work and no play. We went camping and water skiing just like we had when I was little. But he also put his professional experience to work helping me develop a solid business plan.

Meanwhile, while keeping my full-time job in the real estate office, I landed a second job as a cocktail waitress on Thursday and Friday nights from 10 p.m. until 2 a.m. Those two days I left the house at 8 a.m. and got home about 2:30 the next morning. Fridays were pretty brutal. I took my pillow to work at the real estate office and slept in the break room on my lunch hour. I don't think my bosses were super happy about it, but they did respect my drive and ambition.

For all the sleep it cost me, it was my second job that brought me the man of my dreams. I will never forget the night I met John Morgridge outside the club where I was working. He was way too cute and drove a fancy car. At first I wanted nothing to do with him, though we did flirt the night away. After all, I was seeing someone else. The next week, however, I had broken up with the other guy and told John it had been the best week of my life. I was free now, so he could ask me out.

He said, "That's nice."

He tortured me all night during my shift before finally asking me out. I was so excited! I wrote down my phone number on a cocktail napkin (we still have the napkin). Our first date was amazing, but at 10 p.m. John had to drop me off at my waitressing job. He wasn't thrilled, because he didn't want his new girlfriend serving drinks to a bar full of strangers. That was fine with me. I quit my job at the bar and couldn't have been happier.

It was obvious that we had many of the same interests and shared the same values. In 1990, John was flipping houses in Redwood City, and I worked in a real estate office in San Francisco. We spent our second date up in Napa, California, and soon realized we were falling in love. We were married four months after we met. Through all the years and all the adventures since then, we've worked together, played together, and loved together. I have never looked back.

Based on the business plan Dad and I came up with, John believed enough in me to invest in my dream. With that, we opened our first tanning salon, Tropical Solution. Soon we turned one location into the largest chain of tanning salons in the Bay Area.

Before long we were the parents of two wonderful children, John and Michelle. With them in our lives, the future looked a lot different. With the Bay Area getting more congested and our incredible passion for the great outdoors, we asked ourselves if California was really the place we wanted to raise kids.

I wrote to several chambers of commerce to research the cost of living, recreational opportunities, and other information. We finally settled on Aspen, Colorado, where we found a place to live and enrolled the kids in Wildwood Preschool. It was the perfect choice for us because we could spend more time with the kids outdoors and less time in a car on a crowded freeway.

We discovered that the Aspen real estate market was booming. We dove into the Aspen/Snowmass real estate market in the early 1990s buying, remodeling, and selling homes and condos. You really couldn't go wrong in Aspen, and the money was very good.

I had always loved sports and considered myself an athlete; in Aspen I met *real* athletes. We're talking world class. You never bragged about yourself in Aspen because you never knew who might be sitting next to you. One day we would find ourselves on the chair lift with a member of the US Olympic team, or meeting Neal Beidleman, whose famous climb of Mt. Everest is described in Jon Krakauer's book *Into Thin Air* (New York: Anchor Books/ Doubleday, 1998). I discovered road biking and developed a passion for it. It's really hard biking in the mountains at 9,000 feet, but tremendously rewarding.

Aspen is a varied and exciting place to live. Besides world-famous skiing, there are all sorts of art and cultural institutions, and in the Aspen valley, more than five hundred nonprofits. It was during this time that my in-laws set up their private family foundation and invited their children, including my husband, John, to join the board. Being the greatest husband ever, John always made sure that I was part of the giving process. From the beginning he treated me like an equal and made sure that I was very much a part of the grant decisions.

It's easy to write a check. I wanted giving to be more than that. I wanted to donate to organizations that shared my passions, and that would make every dollar I gave them work hard. To learn how to give smart, I called the local community foundation, the Aspen Valley Community Foundation. The board was made up of very talented business people who had been extraordinarily successful in life, and they were some of the most knowledgeable philanthropists in the country. I could learn so much from them.

After several interviews, the board offered me a position with them. I couldn't have been more thrilled. That's where I learned how to be a nonprofit board member, how to go on site visits and write up reports, and how to evaluate a grant request. I took it all in by watching that board debate and plan and strategize growth, impact, and giving. They taught me about a donor advised fund, which allows donors to give anonymously if they wish, and to give a number of gifts by writing a single check. They showed me how to thank people—how to express gratitude for gifts given to the community foundation. I acquired the crucial skill of knowing when a grant just didn't fit the focus of the board and when to say no. I would come home from a board meeting so jazzed that I'd almost be bouncing off the walls!

Despite enjoying my experience with Aspen Valley Community Foundation, it was during this time that we found ourselves in a difficult situation with the local schools. Our children were older now, and we felt the schools weren't meeting our family's needs. We decided it might be time to move to a more mainstream city. So we picked up and moved to Orlando, Florida, trading our snow skis for water skis.

That's when my dear friend and biking/running partner Elliott

Robinson suggested I try an Ironman race. Now that was a crazy idea, but after thinking about it for ten seconds or so I decided, why not?

The Ironman race is a triathlon event that started on Oahu in the 1970s as a friendly competition between the army and the navy. Contestants swam 2.4 miles (the length of Honolulu Bay), biked 112 miles (the distance around the island), and finished by running a marathon (26.2 miles).[6] I trained my heart out in the heat of Florida. I had the support team that I needed: an amazing, loving, supportive husband and two great kids.

On my first attempt, at age thirty-six, I became an Ironman finisher, completing the Panama City race in 13 hours 40 minutes! John trained with me the whole way and the next year he competed too—taking 1 hour and 20 minutes off my time, even with arthritis in his ankle. My dad—who is still a competitive water-skier and went to both of our races to cheer us on—took part in the race himself that third year, at age sixty, and finished in 16 hours 50 minutes. Competition is in our blood, so Dad was inspired to race John and me to the Ironman finish line; my dad, my husband, and I: all Ironman finishers. How cool is that?

Like earning your PhD, completing an Ironman is something no one can ever take away from you. No matter what life throws at you, you are always an Ironman finisher. I feel like I sometimes represent the person who never wins first place. Ironman is that place for me. I have never won, nor have I ever dropped out of a race. I hang in there, suck it up, and finish. To me, Ironman represents the values that run through my core: sacrifice, perseverance, discipline, and commitment.

Now it was time for a new goal. At the very moment I was pondering where to set my sights, my mother-in-law called to ask, "What's your next goal?" Knowing my drive and my love of a good challenge, she suggested I might want to give college a try. That same day, I got a college pamphlet in the mail asking me if I "have what it takes" to be an interior designer. This sang to my heart! I had been remodeling and flipping houses with John in both Aspen and Orlando, but not as a trained designer. This was exactly what I wanted to do.

I started classes that fall. I also started playing tennis six days a week, so I had to stack my classes on Monday afternoon through Tuesday night, then drive home, have dinner with the family, and disappear to do homework and more tennis. The insane pace reminded me of my waitressing days, but I kept it up for eighteen months and graduated from design school *summa cum laude*.

Sometimes things happen in life that don't seem significant at the time but that turn out to be critically important later on. That's what happened to John and me from a mere flat tire. We were making a tough trek around the back side of Pearl Lake, a steep, three-hour, intense mountain bike ride. John got a flat tire and stopped in a shady spot to change it. Unfortunately, his spare was flat too. As I rode home alone to retrieve his bike tube, the situation reminded me of what happens sometimes in giving. You start to get really good at it, you have a clear path, and you know the journey—we knew that this particular ride would be hard in some places—but the downhill ride is fun, rewarding, and exhilarating. Then something happens, a flat, a fall, a mysterious root that makes you go head over heels. It changes your path, and it changes your thinking. That same kind of unexpected development can change the way you give.

That day on the trail around Pearl Lake, we were back on course within half an hour, and didn't have to change our plans all that much. But looking back at our experiences there have been times when a great book, an inspiring speech, or a single person has had such an impact that we changed course. As you encounter changes in your life, you will also find yourself growing in your giving. The greatest and most satisfying adventures are usually the ones farthest off the trail. You don't have to move across country to change course on your giving, but if you do move, it is a great time to think about how you might change up your giving as well.

The cumulative changes and life experiences I've shared here gave me the tools I needed when I stepped into the role as vice president of the Morgridge Family Foundation alongside John. Even though we're a private foundation, we're a 501C-3, which makes us public in some ways—running the foundation per IRS laws and disclosing all grants made through Form 990. I have been given the opportunity to help run a foundation I passionately care about, holding myself and the board to the highest standards. Though I try to run the foundation like a business—often calling our grants "investments"—I try to have fun along the way.

One important lesson I've seen repeated time and again is that a small amount of money invested properly is life changing. We can all make a difference. We can all experience the immense joy of giving. I hope you will learn, as I have, that sharing with others makes us more grateful for everything we have.

Chapter 3

Follow Your Passion

O nce you see what a difference you can make, the next
step is to decide where to put your resources to work.
Whatever events and choices have shaped your life, giving back to others will make it so much more rewarding. The
options are practically endless and potentially overwhelming.
Requests will come at you from every direction every day. Nobody
can respond to every need they are confronted with; you've got to
decide which ones mean the most to you. Finding your passion is
the key to fulfillment.

Invest your gift in something you care deeply about. Otherwise you're not going to stay interested and all your other day-
to-day responsibilities will crowd it out of your life. This means
you'll miss the joy of doing something for others. If you give just
because it's convenient, or because you feel obligated or pres-
sured, then giving quickly becomes a chore. There are plenty of
worthy causes out there that are happy to take your money, but
only a few will capture your heart. Concentrate on those, and

leave the rest to others. Someone else will be as committed to those causes as you are to yours.

If you already recognize the kind of organization you're passionate about supporting, great. If you're not sure, ask yourself some key questions:

- What's your passion?

- What gets you all fired up?

- What problems do you really care about solving?

- What kind of giving do you think will do your community the most good?

- What opportunity is out there to advance your vision for a better world?

- Of all the organizations that work in your area of interest, which ones are likely to use your money most effectively and efficiently?

Once you've made an initial gift, you'll know whether you've made the right choice. If the outcome is good, you'll want to get more involved and encourage your friends to join in. If not, move on to another option. Look at how this donation compares with a successful gift to another nonprofit in the past. If the outcome was negative, would you partner with them again? Do you see yourself taking a leadership position? Are you interested in a long-term continuing relationship? Does the organization and the people they help appreciate your gift? Do they take the time to write a thank-you letter?

Over the years I've been introduced to literally hundreds of nonprofits and other groups who want my support. Though in some cases the scale of the gift is different, you can use this same set of questions to assess a charity before you get involved. (See the expanded set of questions in the Appendix.) Every responsible and successful nonprofit knows that most of their money and volunteer time come from caring, passionate people. If they recognize the value of your investment, they demonstrate the importance of your gift and treat you accordingly.

Building Friendships

Another way to find the right fit is by referral from a friend who shares your interests. Some of our most successful grants have come from suggestions by friends and family. John and I build wonderful new friendships at those nonprofits with people who share our passions. In the best cases, those relationships don't end at the trailhead—it's just the beginning of the journey. The amount of time we can spend with a grantee is time spent making real connections and forging friendships that last. I'm known for inviting new acquaintances on nature experiences that can include physical endurance—to get to know them better. As far as I'm concerned, the more two-wheeled meetings (code for invigorating mountain bike rides) we can schedule in the summer, the better.

The best relationships between giver and recipient develop naturally—not in some deliberate or preplanned way—and involve give and take on both sides. As we give, we learn and gain from these friendships. One great, crazy, and fun example for me is the first close friend we made after moving to Denver, Colorado. Like most cities, Denver has a very small and tightly woven philanthropic community. The Morgridge Family Foundation is known for its investments in education. So when we first moved to Denver, from Aspen, I got a truckload of invitations from nonprofits to make site visits. Site visits I will agree to, "get acquainted" meetings—no. I never accept invitations to coffee, because I already know that these sessions generally end with an awkward ask for money from our foundation. Drinking coffee tells me nothing about an organization; a site visit usually tells me everything I need to know.

A Visit to Vanguard

Inviting me for a site visit is the best way for a nonprofit to grab my interest. For an entire year, my office received a call from a wonderful bubbly man named John Farnam. John was the director and head of development of the newly opened Vanguard Classical School. This school was super innovative. It had classes for newborns whose parents had to get back to work after six weeks, it had pre-K with parenting classes, and more. But most of all it had John. He had gotten my name from two trusted foundation partners, The Piton Foundation and Donnell-Kay Foundation, who told him that I would love Vanguard and that I might consider making an investment in them. We finally had a chance to meet; our partnership and our relationship were absolutely worth it.

Vanguard Classical School is structured to address the complex needs of students living with disabilities while learning side by side with typical students. This innovative approach reflects how education has evolved to treat learners in a group based on their mastery of a topic, not on a stereotype. Vanguard works directly with families to help get students out of a special education track and succeed in a mainstreamed classroom. The power of this model keeps 140 of the 700 students annually from being labeled "special education" and suffering the devastatingly low expectations that come from such a categorical label. When the best interest of the student drives the conversations, the decisions on how to best support that student become crystal clear. This school honors every learner and creates the environment each student needs in order to be successful. The support is in the form of co-teachers—one special education teacher sharing the classroom with a general education teacher—plus on-site physical, occupational, and speech therapy; an audiologist; and a registered nurse. This is the diverse team and approach that is required to level the field and allow all learners to succeed.

When we arrived at the school for our site visit, the typical development group greeted us, whisked us into the office, and gave us a complete overview of the entire concept and facility. Despite my interest and experience in education, I had never been to a classroom with an interactive whiteboard (IWB). This replacement for the old-fashioned blackboard is connected to a computer desktop via projector. More to the point, I had never seen students so incredibly engaged. Students and teachers alike loved its flexibility and convenience. I asked the price of the technology, which at the time was about $7,000 per classroom. It was scalable for the size of our foundation. With John Farnam's enthusiastic approval, I brought friends in our education world to see IWBs in action, including Todd Horn, the headmaster of our kids' school, and Jerry Wartgow, superintendent of Denver Public Schools. They all confirmed my belief that IWBs were amazing tools for teaching.

Accepting a site visit invitation generally means I'm interested in funding something at some capacity. This site visit and the resulting grant became more than that. It opened my eyes to seeing the classroom of the future. The friends and colleagues I talked to were convinced this was a place that our foundation should invest in. But more important, my visit to Vanguard

introduced me to John Farnam. He couldn't get me out of his
school. I brought in people from all over to see how excited and
engaged the students were. This school was really rocking in general, but the technology was over-the-moon great. Had we not
accepted the site visit invitation, I don't know how long it would
have been before we discovered IWBs. It was John Farnam who
orchestrated a transformation in the Morgridge Family Foundation approach to education by opening our eyes to a school where
the focus was completely centered on the student.

Not long after, John informed us that he had decided the
school wasn't the right fit for him professionally and he was leaving. Since that first site visit, John and I had chatted briefly from
time to time, and we'd started to have dinners together, but I
really wasn't interested in more funding for the Vanguard Classical School. We had just bought a building in Denver for the foundation, and I found that most of the time it was just my husband,
John, and I in the building—leaving three empty offices that we
thought at the time we would give out.

I asked John if he would consider running his marketing company out of our building. To our surprise, he said yes. It would
be great to have him nearby. He and his partner Paul had been
actively involved in the Denver community for years and knew
the people and organizations there much better than we did. I
found myself in John's office more and more, bouncing ideas off
him, asking him to sit in on some of our meetings, and asking for
his advice. Working for the Vanguard School and for Goodwill
Industries before that, he saw requests for funding from the other
side of the table and understood how to evaluate and determine
which groups of people seeking our help would be a good fit. As
our relationship grew, so did my interest in having John Farnam
help advise the foundation.

Within days of visiting the Vanguard School, our foundation decided that we had to get involved with the kind of technology we saw in the classrooms and that it was going to be bigger than anything we had ever done before. Using the skills and the educational networks that I had, we formed a grants committee called 21st Century Classroom Collaboration. Our goal was to give interactive whiteboard technology to teachers who were eager to teach in a different way. Of course we invited John Farnam to join the grants committee.

The twenty-first century classroom is defined by the way a teacher delivers content to an individual or group using technology that puts more of the learning focus on the student. Teachers told us that having lessons immediately accessible on an IWB instead of having to write them out meant they had their backs to the students less and more interactive face time with them. Their lessons are ready to go, and now there are so many more opportunities for teachable moments.

We donated thousands of these high-tech boards, because we knew it was the right tool for both teachers and students to accelerate learning and engagement. Teachers have written us many wonderful thank-you cards expressing how they could never teach again without their board. They tell us that the support they received from our foundation, their school district, and their peers has transformed their teaching forever. We saw a giant leap for education starting with 21st Century Classroom Collaboration. Now, a few short years later, classrooms are equipping today's teachers and students with all kinds of devices, including laptops, iPads, 3-D printers, and even laser engravers. Who knows what the next five years will bring into the classroom!

In our first round of funding, only five school districts had applied for this amazing new technology. Our significant gift to these five districts caught a lot of attention across the state. By year three, we had hosted six rounds of technology funding and amazing things were happening. One school district requested one IWB for every sixth-grade classroom, and the grants committee funded their request. All the parents loved the new technology. Their children were excelling in school. But what about the other children's classrooms that had no technology? This led to what Malcolm Gladwell calls the tipping point, the moment when an idea suddenly reaches critical mass and attracts widespread support. The parents felt so strongly about this new technology in the classroom that they voted to pass a special education tax. Within one year, every classroom in the Poudre School District was equipped with technology for the teacher, and, of course, all the students benefited.

Pay it Forward

Technology is wonderful but, just like money, it's a tool and not a solution. Technology will never replace a master teacher. As we got more involved in 21st Century Classroom Collaboration, it became clear that we had to invest in teacher training as well as high-tech equipment. It took a long time to find great training programs and when we did, it was limited to two high-performing public school districts in Colorado. Both of them, Douglas County and Cherry Creek, were the first ones to apply for interactive whiteboards. Those districts were even willing to train teachers to use IWBs for free as a way of thanking us. It was their way of paying it forward—helping others down the road in appreciation for the investments we made in them.

John and I wanted to host the training on a university campus, and we decided the University of Denver (DU) was the ideal place. My husband and I have a great partnership with DU, and I serve on the board of trustees. We were in the process of granting a mega gift for a new building housing the college of education. However, at the time we were two years ahead of the building schedule. The university staff found a temporary home for the training program, and within two years we moved the event into Ruffatto Hall—housing the Morgridge College of Education.

Share Fair

Gradually the idea for teacher training turned into an event we called Share Fair, a series of seminars, how to sessions, speakers, and collaboration. I can't remember now who came up with the name, but it stuck, and the event was a huge success. Our main goals for Share Fair were to celebrate the teacher, recognize that they need more teaching tools, train them to use interactive whiteboards (IWBs) and other innovative equipment, and create a local network for teachers using technology in the classrooms so they could partner with other teachers who were doing the same. We designed this day specifically to be held on a Saturday so teachers wouldn't miss critical time in the classroom, and the event was FREE for anyone who wanted to come and learn.

In the beginning, we had made attendance a requirement for teachers who had won a technology grant for IWBs. Over the years we dropped the requirement. To our surprise, teachers continued to show up for professional development, and they were happy and grateful. The learning was contagious, and I heard one teacher say, "There was learning going on in the halls" (as the teachers shared what they had learned in the classroom). In the weeks following the event, I got the most beautiful thank-you notes and emails. The common theme was that teachers had never been treated so special and with such high regard. More important, Share Fair gave them tools and tips that they could immediately start using in their own classrooms.

We asked our teachers to pay it forward by training the other teachers in their buildings and in their districts. Today Douglas County is still hosting any teacher who wants to be trained, and they continue to vet and share in open source all the valuable lessons for teachers who use IWBs. The Cherry Creek School District women who developed the original Share Fair event for us, Ann and Karen, went on to start their own company that trains teachers on how to integrate technology into their classroom.

We created Share Fair with some core guidelines that are still in place today. Our intent is to treat teachers like business executives at the highest level. Our mission is to thank them with great food, great trainers, innovative topics, and prizes at the end of the day. By year two, there was a natural progression of continuous improvement as we met the challenge of staying one step ahead of the latest classroom innovations.

Share Fair was gaining recognition and earning a very positive reputation. As participants returned to their schools boasting about the amazing things they learned, a flood of teachers called our office requesting invitations to the event. The manufacturers of the whiteboards, SMART Technologies and Promethean, generously gave away one or two boards at each event, and I'm thankful for our long partnership with both companies. Teachers who've won these boards over the years have enjoyed a direct and immediate benefit in exchange for giving up a Saturday to learn how to make their classroom more fun, engaging, and personalized.

Each year it was critical to reinvent Share Fair in some significant way in order to make it better and improve the overall experience for the teachers. In 2013 we decided to add a public side to the event. This was inspired by teachers who wanted to come for the training but had nowhere for their own children to go while they were there.

I was encouraged by some folks to look at the Maker Faire Movement. So we asked a team from Denver to come with us to experience the New York City Maker Faire, which is like a carnival and science fair combined. We invited some teachers and students from a local charter school for low-income kids that we had been supporting. I wanted to see how they would react to the hands-on learning that's a feature of Maker Faire. The results were mind boggling. Teachers saw for themselves how engaged students are as a result of tinkering, hands-on learning, and having the teacher learn side by side with the student. Fantastic as it was, the whole event was just too big for us to bring to Share Fair. So we did what any entrepreneur would do. We created our own modified version of the idea: hands on, brains on, but less carnival, and more science fun.

In further improving the Share Fair event, we hosted speakers like Salman Khan and Dr. Jane Goodall. Both speakers filled the Magness Arena at the University of Denver, inspiring thousands and encouraging students, teachers, and parents. By this time we were flying hundreds of teachers from around the country to an event-packed Share Fair weekend. This caused us to ask ourselves, "What if we took Share Fair on the road?" So, in 2014, we partnered with four other universities across the country and sponsored five events. This prompted us to change the name to Share Fair Nation. We achieved a 400 percent growth in our first year of expanding, and expect to reach nine cities in 2015.

What started for me as a simple site visit to an innovative Denver school developed into a nationwide training program that helps thousands of teachers and students each year. This story turned out the way it did because at the intersection of education and technology I found my passion for giving. I didn't just write a check, I got involved. John and I and the others who've helped us would never have worked this hard if we didn't deeply care about what we were doing. The impact that we experience, and the satisfaction we get from hosting these events, makes us work even harder the next year. This is how I want you to feel. At the end of the day, if you've worked hard for a cause you believe in and done the best you can do, you will know immediately that you've made a difference. None of us has the money to help everyone. But like the boy on the beach with the starfish, you can experience the joy of following your passion and doing your part.

Chapter 4

Finding Common Ground

Information is a key to smart giving. The more you know about the nonprofit you're interested in, the smarter and more effective you'll be as a donor. The Internet delivers a world of information to your fingertips. It's a great place to start, but don't make your decision based only on the Web. Follow up with a site visit, and then combine what you see and feel about a place with the background facts. After vetting hundreds of nonprofits over the past fifteen years, I'm convinced this is the best way to spend your time, and to ensure that your donation dollars get maximum impact for the cause and maximum satisfaction for you.

Find out who's already at work on the issues that you're most passionate about. Your church, your local government, and trusted friends are all good sources of information. It's harder to judge the accuracy of facts on a website, but they can still give you some guidance and direction. Every source you check will lead you to others, and in time you'll have a list of organizations that share your passion.

There are some fantastic search engines available for this research. One that is focused on education is www.SchoolDigger.com, a nationwide resource that provides performance data on most schools in the country. I like to use it to look at the districts we have invested in and compare them to others. It has top-ten lists, bottom-ten lists, and more—and it's easy to use. Another great site is www.GuideStar.org, which is a search engine of non-profits. As they so perfectly describe their mission online: "We know that the best possible decisions are made when donors, funders, researchers, educators, professional service providers, governing agencies, and the media use the quality information that we provide. Those decisions affect our world today and will continue to affect it for generations to come. We are the search engine for nonprofit information."[7]

As you review websites and make calls, you'll get an idea of the attitude of the people who run these organizations. Ask yourself

- Are they committed to their cause?

- Do they act like they know what they're doing?

- Do they answer questions about their organization simply and transparently?

- Do they look diligently for matching grants and other ways to leverage your donation?

- If so, are they the kind of organization you want to partner with?

Whittle the list down to a handful that impress you the most, ones you feel are most in sync with your passion. Though some of this process is based on facts and information, an important part of it is based on your gut. Don't be afraid to rely on your intuition. There's a little voice that hangs near my ear, or sometimes it is in my stomach. This is my subconscious, and I know to listen to it. If it's telling me to give, it usually tells me to start out small, test the waters, and see what the organization can do and what their communication is like. Once all of those are established and a relationship is in place, it's easy to continue funding.

Go on Site Visits

When you find an interesting charity, give them a call. Not only does a phone conversation tell you something about them, but it also tells them something about you. That way both sides get a sense of how good a match the two of you would be.

Yet no matter how excited or impressed you might be as you continue learning about an organization, think about your comfort level of giving before you go on a site visit. I try to be open-minded about the amount I feel comfortable giving. I think about failing. If my first gift to the organization doesn't have the outcomes that we had all hoped for or expected, I know it's harsh, but I consider that a failure. If I had given my full giving budget for the year, I would be devastated and might not want to give again. I recommend that you plan to start small, see what they can do with it, see how good their communication is, and take note of how they say thank you.

After you've made a successful connection by phone and thought through your giving level, pick your favorite prospects and go see them. Meet with the leadership and their development director (the person responsible for raising money) or with other people in charge of fundraising. I know taking time to do this isn't easy. You've already got life pulling at you from every direction, yet here I am telling you to somehow carve out the time to make a visit in person.

In my experience, visiting the site is essential for three reasons. First, any nonprofit is only as good as the people who run it. At the end of the day you're investing in people. The best way to get a feel for the people in charge is to meet them. First impressions are crucial to me as a donor. The first person I meet in an organization sets the tone. If they're not friendly and excited about what they do, I'm not likely to donate to their cause. It's a lot more informative to have a conversation with whoever is carrying out the group's mission than to read about them online. Face-to-face you have a chance to connect that you won't get any other way. Second, you have the opportunity to learn how things work at that particular nonprofit by seeing it in action. The more you know about their process, the better you can help. Third, showing up in person proves that you're interested in learning about them and possibly helping them with your time or your pocketbook. This builds their confidence in you and earns their trust. If you see gaps in their organization and want to make suggestions, they'll be far more willing to listen than if you're a strange voice calling from behind a desk.

A site visit shows me how willing a nonprofit is to do its own homework: gathering information is a two-way street. The more they know about the foundation and me, the quicker we find common ground on a gift. Nothing is more frustrating for me than to talk with someone who is asking us for a grant, for example, and have them start explaining the details related to STEM (science, technology, engineering, and mathematics) education. I know a lot about STEM education, which they would have realized if they'd done a little digging on our foundation. When you're soliciting a gift, do your homework! Don't waste people's time.

Nonprofit's IRS Form 990

Another great source of information is the nonprofit's IRS Form 990. This is both the nonprofit and the private foundation's federal tax return. Simply enter the nonprofit's name in your browser and then "Form 990." It will tell you how much of their money is spent on salaries and fundraising, and how much on programs. You can see their budgets, the compensation of their executives, and lots of other details. When I'm researching an organization other than a school, I find this data helpful. Then when I go on the site visit, I feel prepared to ask intelligent questions.

Love Your Data

About three years ago I attended a presentation from the STEM coordinator at the Adams 12 Five Star School District in Colorado. I went because a teacher I trust and respect told me it would be worth my while. STEM stands for science, technology, engineering, and mathematics, and it defines a curriculum that concentrates on these areas in order to prepare students for careers in tomorrow's technological world. This STEM program also taught the students presentation skills, public speaking, and practical problem solving to help them apply what they knew to real-world challenges. Kellie Lauth opened her speech by illuminating the fact that 90 percent of her students lived below the federal poverty line. Then she explained how she partnered with the local business community to tutor students in writing business plans—beginning in kindergarten! By the time a student graduates from one of Kellie's three STEM schools (which serve as a STEM pipeline in K–12), they've written more business plans than most MBA graduates.

When she stepped off the podium I knew I had to invest in

Kellie and her schools. Surely there was a place for Morgridge Family Foundation to partner with this amazing woman who was turning the K–12 STEM world upside down.

Before going on the site visit, we pulled up the data on her STEM Launch school using SchoolDigger.com. Their math results were the best I had ever read for a low-income neighborhood school. It's unheard of that 93.5 percent of fourth graders were performing at or above grade level in math when almost 90 percent lived in poverty. In fact, the data was so good I shot the link to my data gurus at the University of Denver. They confirmed my belief that I needed to see these schools for myself.

I never like to go on a site visit by myself. I take people I trust with me, because we always see and hear different things. Within a week, John Farnam and I were at Kellie's school. A typical day at STEM Launch starts with an hour and a half of music. All the students were dancing, singing, learning keyboard, or learning guitar. The classrooms were humming with young voices and full of wiggling, giggling, and sheer happiness to be at school. The teachers were engaged and excited and seemed to love being there as much as the kids did. Everything on this visit exceeded my expectations.

What happened next only happens occasionally, but when it does, it's absolutely magical. We sat down with Kellie and her principal and talked about what an investment in her school might look like. I was shocked to learn that I was the first foundation to ever do this. As we sat around the table, I asked my essential questions about what they wanted versus what they truly needed and what we could fund. We also discussed dollar amounts on what my comfort level would be for a first investment. They wanted to achieve one-to-one in technology, meaning that every student would have his or her own technology device to use as a learning tool. At the time, I didn't think I had it in my budget to grant their request. Yet, as we talked through the possibilities, Kellie and her colleague came up with a brilliant plan using iTouch. These are simple, easy to use, inexpensive devices that could be put in every student's hands. The kids could do classwork as well as research for their businesses. We approved the grant on the spot, and within thirty days the entire school had a one-to-one device. Kellie later told me they did a happy dance in the back room. When they announced our gift to the other teachers, they were overwhelmed with tears of joy.

Kellie said that on their first field trip with the new iTouches, the students were texting home to their parents about what they were learning, that they were safe, and that they were having a great time. Three years later this school still uses the iTouch device. The students love them and do all kinds of research and school projects on them. They even used them to make some short movies for summer school. The ripple effect of this gift has reached three years of students, completely exceeding our expectations for the original grant.

As someone who loves data, I look up to one of the biggest disruptors of our time in education—Salman Khan. In education disruption is seen as super positive, because of the work from Dr. Clayton Christensen of Harvard.[8]

You will learn more about him later, but I couldn't talk about statistics without mentioning the power of Khan Academy data and their impressive analytics. Khan Academy developed a platform to provide data to each student. The Academy's free software generates a wealth of individualized information that helps both student and teacher, because it shows where students are in understanding a math or science concept. For the first time ever, students actually know where they are in real time and don't have to wait a week for an old test to be handed back to see what they might need help on. The concept of personalized learning is having a huge impact.

We have teachers share with us that they used to "teach to the middle" because they felt it was their only option. Now, with Khan Academy each student gets exactly what he or she needs at an individualized pace. The teacher can take advantage of that teachable moment, at different times for different concepts. While the whole class is learning, each student moves ahead at his or her own pace. We are seeing the math ceiling—which limited kids to whatever the curriculum and textbook could teach—being lifted from classes, as advanced students are encouraged to move on to higher levels. Some teachers have told us they had no idea that some of their students were gifted until they started using Khan Academy.

Our partnership with Adams 12 STEM Launch school is a case where everything came together. We did our research, got to know the leaders, went on a site visit, identified gaps that we could help fill, and were delighted to see our resources put to use immediately. Not only did the grant help the kids we had targeted, it is also still giving today.

Don't Trust the Averages

Another lesson we learned along the way is to not trust the averages when you're reading data. I was at a breakfast with Mile High United Way and the speaker was the CEO and president of the Annie E. Casey Foundation. The Casey Foundation is known nationally for their work and funding in foster care. The speaker was going through the seven points he had learned along the way and was passing his philanthropic wisdom onto us. I will never forget his fifth point: Don't trust the averages. He shared that the average foster care child moves nine times in one year. But if one child moves only once and finds a forever home, that means the other child who (on the average) moved nine times now moved twenty times.

I can't tell you how important this lesson is. If I had based my decision to go to the STEM Launch school solely on the district's data as a whole, I might not have gone. According to SchoolDigger.com they are currently ranked seventy-sixth out of 126 districts. That puts them in the bottom fourth of the entire state. Most of their students cannot read or write at grade level. We already know and understand that if a student can't read by the third grade, their chances of succeeding in life are severely hindered. But the school's immediate focus is on STEM, and according to their data in the math and science area, they're blowing the doors off!

Why Should You Care About Nonprofit Information?

The website www.GuideStar.org brilliantly states why we should all be so passionate about nonprofits and want to know more about them. It's because nonprofits are incredibly powerful! According to the Center for Civil Society Studies at Johns Hopkins University:

> *"Seventy million people work and volunteer in the nonprofit sector in the United States. Nonprofit employees make up the third-largest workforce among US industries, behind only retail and manufacturing, and nonprofits create a total revenue of more than $1.9 trillion*

annually, exceeding the total GDP of Canada, Australia,
Russia, or India."[9]

   "But nonprofits are so much more than statistics. Col-
lectively, nonprofits make the world a better place. No
matter what their focus, nonprofits touch almost every-
one's life nearly every day."[10]

Don't Be Bullied into a Grant

No matter what focus you choose for giving, there are hundreds,
if not thousands, of organizations doing the same good work. You
can't support them all, so you have to pick one or a handful and
partner with them. It doesn't mean that you don't appreciate the
others, but your time, talent, and treasure can only go so far. The
good thing about a long list of options is that you can change your
mind when the situation requires it.

   A nonprofit founder in Denver called me to share the impact
they were having on low-income students. The program was truly
effective, but it was outside the focus of our foundation. I shared
with the founder that while his organization was amazing, it was
not the right fit for our foundation. Instead of thanking me for
my time and consideration when I declined our support, he gave
me the most shocking and hurtful comment. He said that he
understood that times were tough, implying that the foundation
didn't have any money. I was furious. Not only did this arrogant
man offend me personally, but also he lost me as a donor.

   The lesson I came away with from that day: it is my right and
my duty to the foundation to say no to a grant when it's not the
right fit. My advice when considering gifts of any size is that if it
doesn't feel right, say no. As I've gained experience in listening

to funding requests, I screen meetings harder by asking what they want first, before I will spend an hour listening to a pitch. It is your money, your time, and your life. You have every right to decline a request for any reason you want.

In those exciting and rewarding situations where you do give a donation, don't let your work end with the gift. Follow up. Give them a call or stop in for a visit to see how the organization is doing. You may be able to find out exactly how your contribution was spent. If the money was well spent, keep them on your list and keep giving. If not, kindly say no to their request for future donations and look for another organization to support. Yes, it's tempting to write a check and be done with it. But by giving in that manner, you miss out on so much! Not the least of which is the incredible satisfaction of knowing your money is working to the max and doing exactly what you want it to do.

Chapter 5

Be a Difference Maker

What happens when you have a heart and a willingness to give but don't find an organization that fits what you have in mind? Or you'd rather just move forward on your own? In that case, you start something new! Some of the most inspiring stories I know are about donors with few resources and no important connections who see a way they can make a difference by starting from scratch. One of them began changing the world while he was still in elementary school.

When Kylan was five, he started writing to a pen pal in Uganda named Haruna (a child his family sponsored through World Vision). A year later, Kylan decided to start a business to help Haruna's village. His first idea was a lemonade stand, which didn't turn much of a profit even though he served his customers while wearing a suit and top hat. His next idea was to recycle scrap metal. He distributed flyers in his neighborhood asking for donations, and soon piles of aluminum cans started appearing on his driveway. He collected about $400 in two years. Through the World Vision International, he was able to buy school supplies and livestock such as a goat, sheep, and chickens for the Ugandan village where his pen pal lived.

Kylan thought he could do more if he could get his school involved, so he made business cards for his "company" called Metal Mission and requested a meeting with his principal, my friend Kellie Lauth. He took his new cards and a copy of an article about him in *Quality Digest* that Mark Schmit of the National Institute of Standards & Technology had written the year before. Kylan had wanted to design and build a custom skateboard for his grandfather, a Vietnam veteran, with his military insignia in the design. After raising the money through helping friends and family with yard work and shoveling snow, he partnered with Denver-based KOTA Longboards to design and build the perfect board. KOTA shared the story about partnering with Kylan at his school. That planted the seed for Kids Connection, a popular and growing partnership between local manufacturers and Kylan's school district.

After meeting Kylan, the principal was so impressed that she invited him to speak at the Parent Teacher Organization. When Kylan's story got out, other students wanted to help make a difference in Uganda. Today there are a hundred students in the school who are going to be difference makers in Uganda by helping provide access to clean water, medicine, simple preventives like mosquito nets, and more. Manufacturer's Edge, where Kylan's mother, Sumer, works, has offered to help the students develop new products to improve the quality of life for their African friends.

Kylan is what I'd call a social entrepreneur, someone who comes up with innovative solutions to society's most pressing social problems. These types of entrepreneurs are ambitious and persistent no matter what their age. They tackle major social issues and offer new ideas for wide-scale change. Rather than leaving societal needs to the government or business sectors, social entrepreneurs find what isn't working and solve the problem by changing the system, spreading the solution, and persuading entire societies to move in a different direction.

Kylan's first step was getting his pen pal and building a relationship. Then he saw the need, wanted to help, and got a job to save money for it. He filled the immediate gap by buying chickens and other livestock. Then he raised his sights to long-term solutions.

After she heard his presentation to the Parent Teacher Organization (PTO), Kellie called me to come meet this remarkable kid. By then I was working on this book, and we felt it important to interview Kylan. It was such a great day! After the interview I called my friend Dr. Jamie Van Leeuwen to share how Kylan was making this huge difference for a pen pal and the people in his village. Jamie has his master's degree in international public health and sociology and a doctorate in public policy. He does work in Uganda and I knew he was going there in a few months.

"Would you consider taking Kylan and his mom to Africa to meet his pen pal?" I asked. Of course he enthusiastically agreed. They immediately started a dialogue with World Vision, and on June 6, 2014, Kylan and his mom were approved to go and visit Haruna. World Vision wrote, "We believe that Kylan is already making a difference! Again, thank you for your partnership with World Vision. We are glad to have you come alongside us as we strive to build a better world for children!"

Kylan's mother, Sumer, has told me about additional opportunities they've already uncovered. A logistics company has offered to ship donated goods for free. Johns Manville offered tenting material. Crocs donated crates of shoes. Kylan's spirit and practical results have inspired these and other companies to pitch in and donate in ways that are making a difference.

When he was four, Kylan read about Thomas Jefferson and

Benjamin Franklin, and decided his number-one goal in life was to be in a book too. It took him until he was nine, but now he's finally made it. When his mom asked him what his new goal would be, he said, "Change Uganda." I have a feeling he just might do it. With four years of letter writing under his belt and a trip to Uganda, Kylan came back to school the next year ready to develop new ideas that could change the course of Africa forever. We'll just have to wait and see.

Difference Makers from two continents meet: Kylan and Haruna in Uganda, August 2014.

Students Supporting Students

The members sat in the library debating which grant deserved funding. The conversation was getting heated over who was more deserving of the grant. The school choir that had just won the state competition and now was invited to perform at the national competition, or the single student whose family had received an eviction notice and was days away from living on the streets. One option affecting many people from the school, awarding them recognition with a grant for the trip, to say "Good Job" and congratulations for working so hard to make it to nationals. The other request affecting one student, one family, but a moral dilemma for members of the Student Support Foundation to decide.

John and I have always believed that young people are incredibly passionate and want to do the right thing. So we wondered whether we could teach students how to give away money, using our money for the hands-on experience. I found a public high school that was close to our home in Orlando, Florida, and decided to see if they would be interested in creating a program in youth philanthropy.

There I met a wonderful woman named Nancy Bardoe who thought our idea had legs and might be a good fit for the students at Olympia High School. After many meetings with the school and the students, my assistant and I came up with the idea for an afterschool club.

This club, the Student Support Foundation or SSF, formed its own bylaws, giving guidelines, and governance. They developed their own grant forms and approval and decline letters. As the idea spread to other schools, we encouraged each club to create its own name and logo. They were also encouraged to design tee shirts for school club pride. They established bimonthly meetings and soon started giving away the money we had set aside for them. We asked each club to establish three giving focuses so that they could learn to stay on course with their own giving. They could also decide when it was time to break their own rules. Some clubs support the school nurses, other clubs support the teachers, and many of them have felt strongly about individual grants. The budget each Student Support Foundation club receives from us is $4,000 per year.

Clubs submit an annual report to our foundation, including their budget and balance sheets. They prepare reports to describe the most difficult grant given and the best grant given. They submit details about their fundraising project and how much money they raised. Finally, we ask that each school design a green project of their choice, either supporting an environmental project at their school or a new program that protects or promotes the environment. Students call the shots. We found that when we're 100 percent hands-off, the students excel. They know their own community and where needs are not being met.

Since the clubs started ten years ago, we have expanded to many states. In our continuous improvement plan, each club is now required to raise money, participate in or fund a green project, and recruit new club members each year. We've also added two colleges to our long list of high schools where SSF clubs are thriving.

The college model is different from the high school clubs, but only slightly. Both colleges, Plymouth State University and Rollins College, found that the biggest need on each campus was actually food. Some students just run out of food before the end of the year or are supporting families while putting themselves through college. Each campus has started its own food pantry, and this year the professors were so touched by what the students were doing they decided as a group to support the food pantry as well.

Student Support Foundation club members at Rollins College

are tackling some difficult life issues too, and they are becoming social entrepreneurs at the same time. In their latest report, they shared with me that they were:

> ". . . *able to provide to a single mother of two who had recently overcome a serious case of domestic violence. We granted her $200 for food and living costs to allow her to continue her education, while also supporting her family. Her case really inspired us, as she is now a leading advocate on the Rollins campus for promoting awareness about domestic violence and providing support to victims of abuse. For our members it was an important educational lesson to understand that we have peers in dire need in our community. These students blend in, but hold stories of such great personal fortitude and resiliency. This particular grant represented this important lesson for our club members and reminded us of the importance of this organization in developing a more inclusive, accessible, and healthy community.*"

One of the SSF grants at Plymouth State University was for a student who was on the verge of dropping out of college. He had not had a new pair of reading glasses since the eighth grade, and it was almost impossible for him to read all the college-level required reading. He applied to SSF club and received not just one pair of glasses but two! With help from the club's $100 investment, this student went on to graduate.

One year, one of our high school clubs reported that its most exciting and rewarding grant had been awarded to the hardest working SSF board member. This student worked her tail off for the club and was so passionate about SSF that she almost never missed a meeting. When the time finally came to select grantees she had to admit to the club she was actually one of the students in need. She asked for a special board meeting, submitted her story, and excused herself. The club deliberated for hours over whether or not to fund her request. They even called me to weigh in on whether donating to a club member was ethical or not. After hearing the full story my response was, "Rules are meant to be broken." I was thrilled when the club sponsor called me back to share that the students unanimously chose to fund this very special grant request.

The best part of creating Student Support Foundation for me is what I get to learn every year. I learn how passionate students are for their own school, their community, and helping one another. I learn that by trusting the students—completely hands-off—they exceeded my expectations of becoming responsible and caring philanthropists themselves.

Students at Olympia High School where the first Student Support Foundation began over a decade ago.

Start Something New

When you're looking for a program or a nonprofit to support, you might find yourself in a dilemma because what you are looking for doesn't exist. Social entrepreneurs of all ages tackling all kinds of issues are right there with you. Follow their lead and take the first step: create something new. You might just find yourself transforming an old organization with your brilliant new ideas.

There are difference makers of all ages in your community if you look in the right place. At Cracker Trail Elementary in Sebring, Florida, the first-grade class was inspired by their teacher to do a community service learning project. Using Jane Goodall's Roots and Shoots mapping program, which encourages kids to explore and map natural features in their neighborhoods, the class decided to do their project on the Florida black bear. Their goal was to teach their community to peacefully coexist with the bears that shared their environment. The students held a campaign event at the PTO Hoedown, featuring delicious edible "cubcakes" decorated to look like bears. The students even wrote letters to their local Publix grocery store and were awarded a $100 gift card. They brought in a bear biologist, made tee shirts, and went on a field trip.

The students did such a great job that they were invited to present their story to Jane Goodall herself on her eightieth birthday.[11] They named their campaign the Neigh-BEAR-hood Watch program. They even came up with stickers for trash cans, which they called Trashcan Tattoos, reminding people to dispose of trash properly. Their work has caught national attention from being featured on Jane Goodall's eightieth birthday Google hangout and in *National Geographic*. The Be Bear Aware campaign in Missoula, Montana, heard about the project and sent the first-grade class over $500 worth of materials. To celebrate the success of their project, the students had a Teddy Bear Picnic on the school lawn with their teachers and families. Did I mention that all of this started with a $200 grant from our foundation? These students and teachers have exceeded our expectations for conservation in a fun new way.

All of these innovative and hard-working students are what I would call difference makers. Given the opportunity, time, and talent, and seeded with a touch of money, these students are making a difference. We see this kind of giving having a profound impact for a small amount of money. Look for difference makers to support in your community. Or become one yourself!

Chapter 6

Full Circle

W hen I look at the world I see a series of circles—circles of relationships, of events, of cause and effect, of students growing into teachers. To me, the experience of giving is a process of moving through these circles. Sometimes I'm teaching, and other times I'm learning. I may be giving advice or receiving it. A person or an organization can start out as a recipient of one of our foundation's grants and in time turn into a trusted advisor. I have found myself time after time asking past grantees for their insights on a new gift and leveraging their experience and expertise. It's all part of completing the circle.

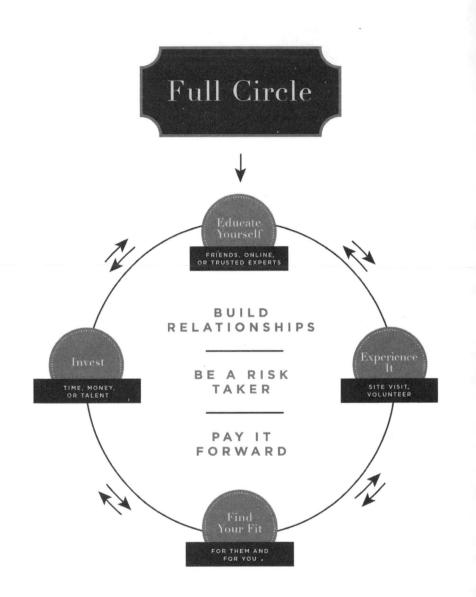

From Failing to Fantastic

Since our foundation is known in the Denver community for its commitment to education, we get a lot of calls for help from local school districts. In 2010 a request came from the Englewood School District near our office. They were a failing district and had employed ten different superintendents in the past nine years. The State of Colorado was going to take over this district if they did not turn it around.

Fifty-five percent of the students were minority, and at some schools nearly 90 percent of the kids qualified for free or reduced lunches, which indicates they live at or below the official federal poverty level. In addition, at one of their elementary schools only 31 percent of the third-grade students could read at grade level

As a prospective donor, you can react in two different ways to data like this: run the other way, or knuckle down and embrace the opportunity. The Morgridge Family Foundation took the second path.

I agreed to meet with them, but at our initial meeting the superintendent wasn't there. I sent the others home and told them to come back when the superintendent had time to talk. Within a week, the superintendent, Brian Ewert, appeared in my office. I was interested to hear how he might turn around his district, and what they needed from us to do it.

Brian Ewert quickly won me over. This was a new team, and they were all committed to turning the district around. We began a fruitful conversation about the various problems and what it would take to tackle them. Over the next two hours, Brian and his colleagues explained why the district was in crisis and where they needed the most help.

We set up a series of monthly meetings to examine failing programs and look for possible solutions. During these meetings, we would discuss the immediate needs of the district, what might be reasonable for our foundation to fund, and what the district would have to fund. Together we built a strategy with Englewood Schools to move forward.

If we were to turn the district around, we had to invest in programs with an immediate impact. One of our first grants was to improve literacy. We selected a web-based reading intervention program called Reading Plus, which works at each student's individual pace. Morgridge Family Foundation had been funding this program for years and it had a good track record that could be scaled. Englewood did their research and agreed this would be the perfect program to jump-start their district. Getting kids to read at grade level became a top priority.

To add incentive, we offered free laptops to the kids who made the most improvement every month. This was a powerful encouragement and one that was affordable to implement because we gave one computer per month per school. This allowed fourteen students to earn a computer every month of the school year.

We planned to give out the prizes at the school board meetings. Little did we expect this would attract huge numbers of parents and family members to the meetings. For some students, it was the first award they'd ever won. Their families and friends flocked to the meetings, sometimes taking five rows of seats to see their beloved child win an academic award and a laptop. After the first couple months, the school board had to move the meetings to a bigger place. What started out as a program to help students and give them incentive also got their parents interested in the school board and actively engaged in their child's school.

Englewood's director of information technology, Mike Porter, attended our monthly planning meetings and soon became one of our expert advisors on classroom technology. Mike has a cheery disposition and somehow can always explain technology down to my level of understanding. It's like Mike is a translator of a foreign language. I find technological language to be confusing, and Mike is there for us as an expert and guide, converting meaningless technobabble into plain English.

Turning Full Circle

As the results grew with Englewood Schools, our trust grew along with it. Occasionally I relied on Mike to come with me on other site visits to offer his expertise. But, more important, Mike was there to provide his much-appreciated technology translation services.

A dear friend of mine in Denver, Christie Isenberg, called to suggest a school she thought would be a good fit for our foundation's philanthropy goals. Tennyson Center for Children, founded in 1904, turned out to be far more than a school. It's a very special place where children are given back their childhood after the trauma of abuse and neglect. Children come to Tennyson with very few possessions, but lots of memories—most often of tragedy, trauma, and fear. This story from their website puts their work in perspective:

> *When ten-year-old Andrea came to Tennyson Center for Children, the treasures she brought with her were few. In her backpack she carried a stuffed animal she loved, a school paper with a high grade, and a few other cherished possessions. This sweet girl had virtually no family. Her stepfather, who had molested her repeatedly, was now in prison. Her mother struggled to be the kind of parent she always wanted to be and was homeless at times.*[12]

Some of the children live at the Tennyson Center and others arrive from all across the state for therapeutic treatment and education. The school at Tennyson is an integral part of the treatment process, as most of these children have had little or no academic success as a result of their family situation. The compounded impact of abuse and failure in school is so destructive. If little Joey is beaten up by the neighborhood gang and his mother is in jail, school might be the only place he has a chance to succeed. Tennyson works to repair the damage by stabilizing the family and diligently attending to the children's academic needs as their situation improves. This school had asked Christie if the Morgridge Family Foundation might be willing to help them improve their educational services.

Before we went on the site visit to see this school, they had informed us that they needed help with classroom technology. The reason our foundation has become so passionate about funding technology for classrooms is that we've seen firsthand how technology improves students' performance by allowing them to learn at their own pace. No matter where a student starts out academically or what skills he or she has, a master teacher coupled with the right tools can accelerate the learning for every child. Technology alone is not the silver bullet, but it can help disadvantaged students catch up with their peers. Through our work with Mike Porter, we asked him to join us on this site visit as our consultant. By this time, he had come full circle from requesting a grant to being our expert in assessing new grants.

The teachers at Tennyson began the meeting by telling us that the students generally come in one to three years behind their peers. Along with many other items on their wish list, the school administration wanted our help closing technology gaps in their curriculum. We started going down the list and asked them to put items in order of priority. Our foundation is nimble enough to say yes to grants right on the spot, and as they spoke we highlighted what our foundation *could* fund, without letting them know yes or no. At the end of the meeting our foundation was able to say yes to most of the items they were asking for.

The team from Tennyson looked at us speechlessly. After a long beat of silence one of them said, "What?!"

"We can give you most of what you need. Immediately."

They all started crying. Then I started crying. As we finished our meeting that day, the room was filled with tears of joy, hope, and optimism. I still get goose bumps from that special moment, and it all happened because a trusted friend led the way, a trusted expert helped, and a loving husband gave me the power to say yes! Within twenty-four hours we sent the school a check so they could start ordering what they so desperately needed.

There's another full-circle journey in the story. Mike Porter, who knew personally about both the power of technology and the impact of a Morgridge Family Foundation grant, offered to give the Tennyson School the old broadband network from Englewood. Mike said this was his way of paying it forward to all of us at the Morgridge Family Foundation for what we'd done for his school and his district. As he told me, Mike has seen the benefit of a well-targeted investment firsthand, and was ready to do whatever he could to help other educators make the most of leading-edge technology. Another thing that Mike shared from his point of view—"One of the implicit values of the Morgridge Family Foundation is that all of us, donors and grantees alike, are part of a community, and that community takes care of each other." From recipient to expert advisor, Mike is a shining example of gifts going full circle.

Closing the Relevance Gap

There's a huge gap between what many schools teach and what today's business economy needs. You met my friend Kellie Lauth a little earlier. Her STEM Launch school curriculum closes this relevance gap, as I noted, by teaching practical problem-solving techniques. Students know more than facts; they know how to learn, how to analyze, how to think critically, solve problems, and achieve results. Not only are the students learning basic education skills, they're also learning how to launch businesses and become entrepreneurs. Kellie has developed a meaningful partnership with the local Boulder business community, which is full of think-tank serial entrepreneurs. The CEOs and CFOs from these businesses evaluate the students' business plans and their start-ups—starting in kindergarten.

At a presentation I attended, a STEM Launch fourth grader told his audience why his first three businesses failed. He said he knew much more now than he did in third grade, and he was betting that his new company would be a real success.

Music is threaded throughout the fabric of the STEM school. There is nothing more special than walking into a first-grade music room where all the students are dancing, singing, snapping their fingers, and loving being at school. At Kellie's schools, all students are required to play the piano and the guitar. When you stop focusing on standardized tests and you have a great plan for all students to learn, learning happens! Education experts Yong Zhao and Sugata Mirta both stress this point explicitly in their many TED Talks videos.

Once we met with the leaders of STEM, it was obvious that we should invest in a strategic partnership. The success of the partnership moved Kellie from grant recipient to our STEM expert—as well as our friend. We didn't anticipate that Kellie would become part of our foundation family, but that's one of the joys of having your gift come full circle.

The students at Kellie Lauth's school rehearsing for the Spring soirée talent show and proving the arts can be integrated into STEM education.

The Counterclockwise Circle

These are only a few of the ways giving can come full circle. People and organizations that come to you for help eventually become your expert advisors in helping others. Groups you donate money and services to end up supporting other groups down the line. Some of these circles may go on indefinitely. And with each turn of the wheel, a cycle of giving and receiving serves another level of grantees and brings you another burst of satisfaction knowing that what you are doing is making a difference.

As I was working on this chapter I saw I had often experienced these full-circle moments without fully realizing them. The concept became clear only when I started putting it down on paper. When I asked Kellie Lauth to review this chapter, her first response—without batting an eyelash—was, "Want to hear our full circle of you?"

Honestly, I had never thought that the foundation and I might form a full circle from the recipients' point of view too. I was both excited and scared to hear her response. I can be brutally honest, I demand the best, my expectation bar is set incredibly high, and I have no problem demanding our foundation's money back if the grantee does not do exactly what was outlined in the agreement—I was afraid my circle might have a flat spot.

But no. Kellie said, "We now use your high level of demands. If a supplier doesn't step up for my district, we dump them. We invest more slowly and gradually, and if the education program works for the class or grade we initially test it on, then we buy it for the entire district." She added, "I love that you understand the value of people and take time to get to know the people you're investing in. We trust you as much as you trust us." We have become each other's full circle.

When we recently needed someone to look at a new pre-K reading program, Kellie immediately put it to use in her school. The results were astonishing. Students were reading better and loving it. Reading performance went up by 20 percent in a single year on state standardized tests. Without experts like Kellie, we couldn't share the data on what is working with our other partnering districts. Having an expert on the inside of education creating data that others can use is incredibly powerful. It's just one more step in the journey of receiving a gift, sharing with others, and paying it forward—that completes the full circle.

Chapter 7

A Seat at the Table

In *The Generosity Network: New Transformational Tools for Successful Fund-Raising* (New York: Deepak Chopra Books, 2013) by Jennifer McCrea and Jeffrey C. Walker, there's a chapter about Jeffersonian dinners. These are dinners where President Thomas Jefferson invited twelve people from different disciplines and viewpoints to discuss important topics of the day. Then he would ask three or four provocative questions that the entire table would discuss in depth. Jennifer and Jeffrey's book had such an impact on me that I immediately set up two Jeffersonian dinners of my own. These really excited me, because I love to hear other people's opinions and very different points of view about important issues.

My ultimate goal at these dinners is to end with this question: "What is the next step?" Turning ideas into action is what great giving is all about for me: the hope and anticipation that something may happen the next day, or it may happen a year down the road. What's most important is that these dinners can spark new passions and some dinners have the power to change our foundation.

Years ago, John and I were invited to a Jeffersonian dinner at the home of Denver Mayor John Hickenlooper—who has since gone on to become the governor of Colorado. The conversation around the table was robust, and I met very interesting people. One person in particular, Roxane White, was absolutely fascinating. At the time, she was manager of the Denver Department of Human Services for the State of Colorado and served on the mayor's cabinet. I was intrigued by the work she had been doing to address homelessness. Roxane had spent sixteen years developing outcome-based programs for homeless youth. It was not our funding focus, and, to be honest, I knew nothing about homelessness. Regardless, Roxane soon invited us to her office for a briefing on the subject. Within a week, John and I found ourselves at the offices of Denver Human Services. This particular meeting would change our foundation and our giving forever.

Roxane created and chaired Denver's Road Home, a ten-year plan to end homelessness. In 2006 she hired Jamie Van Leeuwen, a bright young staffer with a doctorate in public policy, as the project manager. Working together on Denver's Road Home, they generated millions of dollars in funding and new resources for the homeless, reducing overall homelessness by 11 percent and chronic homelessness by 36 percent.[13]

Roxane invited Jamie to join us for our first meeting about homelessness. Jamie was impressive and articulate. Like Roxane, he knew the complexities of homelessness and was willing to spend time teaching us how philanthropy and government could partner to achieve better outcomes for the neediest people. Jamie invited us on a site visit and asked us to support the mayor's plan to end homelessness.

I have to admit we didn't jump at the chance right away to do a site visit. We really wanted to learn about the issues. Jamie made sure to take time to explain the process they had gone through to write the plan. It was a data and fact gathering process: Who was doing what? Who did they serve? What was the outcome? What was the leverage? And so on. Once the strategic plan for Denver's Road Home was in place, then and only then could thoughtful funding begin.

I was afraid of funding homelessness issues. First, I was afraid that once other organizations found out what we were funding the floodgates of grant requests would come streaming in. That didn't happen. I was afraid that we weren't a big enough foundation to make a difference. I was still learning about all the issues and felt vulnerable because I knew so little. But putting my fears aside, at least for the time being, both John and I went on that site visit. Jamie had paid attention at our prior meeting and had been looking for a good fit for the foundation. He knew we cared deeply about children and low-income families. Jamie took us on a tour of a newly opened medical clinic started by doctors from Children's Hospital in Denver. The clinic was set up for the community— serving many families, single parents, and lots of children. In his first introduction of homeless issues for funding to our foundation, Jamie hit it spot on. The clinic was a special place where no one was turned away for lack of payment.

Both Roxane and Jamie took the time to listen to what our foundation's passion was for giving. John and I agreed that their recommendation was the right fit. Our first investment went to the medical clinic, where I was glad to see our grant money put to good use right away. Putting a gift like this to work quickly is essential for us. Time has an impact on the effectiveness of a gift, and there's no excuse for wasting a single second.

We learned more about issues affecting the homeless, such as[14]

- 4,904 men, women, and children are experiencing homelessness in Denver

- 34 percent of respondents are female

- 15 percent are veterans

- 23 percent are working

- 709 of these individuals are chronically homeless (defined as long-term or repeated homelessness, often coupled with a disability)

Employees for Denver's Road Home know these 709 people by name. They know where they live (most of them on the streets or under a bridge). They check in on them often to make sure they are as safe as possible. It is important to note that there is housing available for this group specifically; however, it is their right not to move into assisted housing.

At the same time we were learning about homelessness in Denver, Jamie started taking students from the University of Denver to experience the slums of Kampala in East Africa. These trips were designed to open their eyes and their thinking to issues here at home and how they might approach poverty in a completely different way. The students returned with a burning desire to reduce homelessness in their own city. In his first year, Jamie took eighteen students. Five years later, more than three hundred students, friends, and philanthropists have made the journey to Africa. All of them have come back to America resetting their thinking about what our society needs and how to help.

For me, learning about local homelessness issues was so big

and so complex it honestly felt like the issues of East Africa; too big for one person to make a difference and just too hard. One night at dinner with Jamie just after his return from an African trip he shared with me, "I learned how important it is to rethink and recalibrate how we talk and how we work together. I learned that we need to invite new people to the table if we're going to think differently and if we're going to think big. We need all people at the table if we are going to find innovative solutions to poverty." This is where my friend Jamie advised me that if I am going to improve my own philanthropy I should think about who is sitting at the table. Am I asking the people I am trying to help, "What do you need, what do you want, what would make your situation better?"

His work in East Africa led Jamie to realize Denver's Road Home needed to reset the table for their own homeless neighbors. Maybe it was time to reset our table too.

The notion of resetting the table is what I think about when we at the foundation ask for a transformative grant request. We are asking organizations to think differently about how they approach a problem and, subsequently, how they would approach the solution.

It took five years of hand-holding (a visual term I love to use) for me to fully understand and absorb the complexities of homelessness. As my confidence and knowledge grew, it became clear to me that the foundation could make a positive impact in homeless causes. This is how we became partners, friends, and colleagues with Roxane White and Jamie Van Leeuwen.

During these five years with Jamie, we were introduced to many other funding partners who were doing the same work in homeless causes. Another one of those people we gravitated toward was Jerene Peterson of Mile High United Way. At one point, she had been Jamie's boss (yes, professionals who deal with homelessness are a very small group).

Jerene sat us down and explained that what we had been learning for the past five years could be a starting point in foster care. At that moment, when we had enough experience giving to homeless causes and some wonderful successes with funding and partnerships, we were ready to take a risk to see if we could have a small yet meaningful impact on foster care. Jerene advised us where she wanted to start, and we used the Denver's Road Home process to move in that direction. We all agreed it would be advantageous to start with our partner Jamie and have him help us with a report of where things were and what could be done. We then took Jamie's plan to our foundation partners, the Annie E. Casey Foundation. This report and work lead us into a three-year pilot between Morgridge Family Foundation and Mile High United Way.

What Jamie had taught all of us is that everyone involved in foster care needed more than a simple seat at the table: the whole system needed a reset to think differently about how they approach the problem and consider new ways of helping the children and adults they serve to reach their human potential. This was what our three-year pilot was designed to do.

Our initial funding of this pilot supported a program called Bridging the Gap (www.unitedwaydenver.org/bridging-the-gap). This program does exactly what it says for youth who are exiting the foster care system. If you are sixteen years old or older and have not found a forever home, the program makes it possible for you to live on your own. Bridging the Gap helps these students with wrap-around services—everything from friendship, love, guidance, housing, and food to earning a high school diploma or GED and entering college.

Another gap the initial report identified was a teacher's ability to see and understand their foster care student(s)—to understand what they were going through beyond what was happening at school. Our pilot funded the creation of a new position that would, for the first time ever, have access to both Health and Human Service (HHS) records and Colorado Department of Education (CDE) records. In the first year, this newly trained woman went out into the districts and taught schools not just about the educational needs of the students they were serving but also about the social and emotional services the students needed.

At the same exact time, our federal government had approved policy to directly and positively impact the same group of youth we were trying to help. The most aggressive policy piece to affect this group of kids is called the McKinney-Vento Homeless Education Assistance Improvements Act. This Act conferred specific educational rights to homeless children, including immediate enrollment, records transfer, and transportation to school of origin. It provides additional educational support to homeless children. Working together, nonprofits, local, and federal programs will finally give these young people a better chance at reaching their human potential.

———•———

Inviting people to participate in mapping out their future doesn't always look like you think it will. Our big, interlinked, complicated society overlooks some of its stakeholders in ways we don't realize right away. In American education, the more affluent students have access to education that prepares them for well-paying jobs. Poor students in a poor educational environment are often stuck on paths that lead to a lifetime of low wages. Closing the achievement gap might be the next biggest social injustice that America faces. Robert Goodman is working to change just that. He is the executive director of the nonprofit New Jersey Center for Teaching and Learning. I met Bob at the Global Education Technology Summit in 2011. His data showed that, given an equal chance, every student could learn physics. In his presentation he explained how physics isn't offered in most schools, and only the rich have access to physics classes.[15]

Then Bob showed a graphic that made me laugh out loud. It explained how physics came to be sequenced in the science curriculum. It is taught usually at the end of high school. In 1892 when the basic biology-chemistry-physics sequence was established, the connections between the sciences were unknown. It'd be another decade before quantum physics showed the physical basis for chemistry, and sixty years before the molecular basis of life was revealed, along with its connections to physics and chemistry. In 1892, Algebra I was an advanced course taken by few students and only in the later years of high school. So, botany and zoology were taught, and then chemistry, with few students taking physics (if they first took algebra, which was needed to understand physics). That made sense then.

Now, Algebra I is an essential course for all eighth- or ninth-grade students. Successfully completing Algebra I is the second-best predictor of whether a student will graduate high school and college.[16] It is well accepted that physics is the basis for chemistry and that physics and chemistry are the basis of biology. Taught in that sequence, science makes sense. However, schools are locked into a science sequence that is more than a half century out of date. What we know now is that in scientific learning, sequence matters. Schools continue to follow a decision that became obsolete more than half a century ago due to the incredible inertia of our system of education, which is making our country uncompetitive in the world and depriving many of our citizens the chance for rewarding careers.

Why does all this math and science stuff matter? When you create access for every student to study physics, chemistry, and biology, you produce a graduate who is a talented, well-prepared addition to the workforce and who has the skills today's employers are looking for.

After sitting in on his presentation, I chased Bob down and begged him to come to Colorado. We had technology. The gap we had was that we needed physics teachers. Not only was the New Jersey Center for Teaching and Learning creating free online editable course materials for teachers to use in their classes, it also had the teacher-training component built in.

As I got to know Bob, he shared with me that his high school guidance counselor discouraged him from taking any further math classes, saying he just didn't have what it takes to do math well. Bob took his advice and became an English major. As a freshman at New York University he was required to take one science and one math class . . . and discovered physics. The next year, he took only math and physics, five courses in each, got the highest grades in all of them, and then transferred to MIT for his junior year. He received his physics degree from MIT and had his undergraduate research published by the prestigious *Journal of Applied Physics*. You can see from this example why Bob doesn't believe in tracking students (assigning students to certain tracks), but he does believe in teaching them all. No one, not even the student, knows a student's potential.

Bob decided against a career in research because it would

be too isolating, instead, he entered the audio industry. His twenty-year career included being president and CEO of two top US audio companies—Harman Kardon and JBL Consumer Products—as well as Japan's Onkyo International Operations. After retiring from business, Bob taught in a small private school—at first as a volunteer. When he asked which physics class they would like him to teach, they handed him a huge book and said, "All of it!"

After he stopped laughing, Bob realized that because no teacher could teach all of that, teachers were teaching what they liked, creating incoherence in math and science education.

Later Bob was hired to teach at a vocational-technical high school in New Jersey and was able to put his beliefs about the importance of coherence in math and science education into action. He led the creation of a comprehensive approach to science and mathematics education, which became the Progressive Science Initiative (PSI) and the Progressive Math Initiative (PMI). His system is based on mastery of the concepts, not a one-time test. It uses peer-to-peer teaching where students encourage each other. He never doubted his students could succeed under the right circumstances. Many of the students in Bob's vocational high school have gone on to top universities including MIT, Harvard, Princeton, Yale, and Wellesley. In fact, at least two of the five students who went on to MIT had been told they were not good enough in mathematics to take Algebra I in eighth grade, but they later graduated from MIT with computer science degrees. Just as Bob had done, his students had exceeded expectations, showing that tracking is not a valid approach.

BERGEN TECH STUDENT, LARISA BERGER, MIT CLASS OF 2012

It wasn't until high school that I thought I could be good at math. Physics provided a concrete framework that contextualized concepts I was learning in my algebra and geometry classes. Most of all, Bergen Tech didn't over-complicate learning. My town's public school district became superficially competitive in middle school. While I was a top student, I was placed out of eighth grade algebra and forced to repeat pre-algebra even though I had passed that class the previous year. At thirteen years old I assumed something was wrong with me. I didn't realize that the math I was being taught in the wealthy suburban district in which I grew up wasn't math, it was painting by numbers. I was surprised that I even got into Bergen Tech's engineering program. I fell in love with physics as a freshman because it finally provided context for the logic puzzles I was interested in solving. It was a new way to formalize an idea, not far off from the thinking required to form a persuasive argument in an essay. Most of all, physics provided a method for abstract thinking. This became invaluable once at MIT. While I entered a new domain (computer science) I still was continuing to build upon the problem-solving skills I began developing in algebra-based physics as a freshman in high school.

I've heard some version of my story repeated by many women at MIT. For a long time they identified as qualified only in the humanities, and only because of some freak accident, or more likely the luck of finding an amazing teacher, did they realize they could be just as capable in STEM fields. Imagine what could be possible if we weren't just the exception?

In 2006 Bob was named Teacher of the Year for the state of New Jersey. What he was able to accomplish at a vocational school in physics far exceeded all the private and public schools in the state. He changed the culture; he reset the table. Under Bob's initiatives, New Jersey public schools with high minority populations and high poverty rates went from not offering physics to leading the state in the percentage of students taking the Advanced Placement Physics Test. By 2012, six of the top twelve schools in the state were schools using PSI to teach physics to all students. Those students were taught by teachers who had learned physics, and how to teach it, the same way Bob taught his students. This approach to creating new physics teachers has made his program the number-one producer of physics teachers in the nation!

According to Goodman, "All students must learn math and science to have a fair chance at the jobs of the future. This is essential to the life of each student and this is essential to the future of their country; each country must realize the potential of all its citizens."

This is a national problem. In New York City, half the high schools don't offer physics at all, and only about 20 percent of the students take physics. A few years ago Bob was told that Providence, Rhode Island, only had one physics teacher . . . one for an entire city. When you realize that physics is the science that is required more than any other (more than biology, chemistry, earth, etc.) for careers in medicine, science, engineering, computer science, technology, etc., the lack of opportunity provided to our students is a crisis. If you're in an urban school in the US, chances are you're not being prepared for the work of the future.

It is no surprise that after we put Bob's concept to work in Colorado, we began to see the same success that New Jersey enjoyed.

In two years, thirty-nine teachers have completed training to teach using Bob's techniques, and about three hundred more are learning his methods.

The largest application of the Progressive Math Initiative is in the Adams County School District 50, where eleven thousand students are using the system. Additional schools are joining them so that twenty thousand students in all will soon be in the program. This is a district that was in danger of being closed by the state for repeated poor performance. The Morgridge Family Foundation made a $100,000 gift to the initiative, which the school district matched. The result was that instead of closing down the school, students showed a significant gain in a single year. This kind of improvement is almost unheard of in public education.

Not only did these kids not have a seat at the table before Bob came along, they were also about to lose their table! Hard work, good planning, and partnering with other equally dedicated members of the team—the school district and us—changed the outcome to a degree we scarcely dared imagine. And that investment of time and money will continue to pay dividends in the lives of eager young learners for years to come.

Chapter 8

Invest in Leaders

W hen you're doing your research on which charities to support, it's only natural to focus on each
organization and all the activity and work that
happens with their programs. But one of the most important
lessons I've learned over years of giving is that a surefire way to
spend wisely is to support the *people* in charge. Find great leaders, invest in their work, and hold high expectations. That's when
you'll see real results.

John and I love to invest in ways that spark a change—change
the thought process, change the program, empowering the individual to change. These are places where the leadership is always
innovative, creative, willing to try new things, and dedicated to
working their tails off for something they believe in. We don't
generally put money into operational budgets and usually don't
fund any one recipient for more than three years. That allows us
to start or support specific, well-defined programs and track their
progress, then let them move forward on their own strength.

Certainly many other needs are critical to the organizations, and there are other donors who love giving to operations; it's just not our passion. We try to make this very clear to people who ask us for grants or who apply to the foundation.

When we started giving, we began by searching for the non-profits that fit our interests. At first I didn't pay too much attention to who was running the shop because I seemed to be more interested in the program itself. I wish I had paid more attention to the leadership. I know now that more than anything else, success hinges on visionary, energetic leadership. If I'd learned this lesson years ago, I think the foundation would have made fewer funding mistakes. By mistakes I mean money spent doing less good than it could and should have. Experience has taught me to invest in great leaders who are in various positions throughout the organization.

Leadership comes in many forms, from the head of a non-profit to the CEO of a big corporation, from the members of a strong and visionary nonprofit board to the actual person on the ground. The title people have is less important to us than the passion they have for leading the charge and inspiring everybody around them to achieve greater success. In the world of public education, often it's the teachers who are the model leaders dedicating themselves to innovation in the classroom.

I think of investing my dollars in a nonprofit organization just like I would invest in the stock market. "Is strong and forward-looking leadership present in the boardroom and in the executive suite?" is one of the most important questions you could ask. Others include, "Is there a clear and well-articulated vision of their goals and a strategy to achieve them?" "Do they set a high bar on ethics and risk management?" "Have the leaders demonstrated the ability to produce a solid and consistent return on investment

(ROI)?" The answers identify the hallmarks of top-performing executives *and* top-performing leaders in the nonprofit world. The star performers are the ones who will be good stewards of your hard-earned money.

One key difference between investing in a big corporation and in a nonprofit is that you have a much better chance of meeting the leaders of the nonprofit in person. Nothing is more exciting—or more informative—than sitting down face-to-face with the people in charge. You'll learn far more about them around a table or at their own office than you will during a phone call or an exchange of email. The fifteen years and ten thousand volunteer hours I've invested in nonprofits have given me a lot of face time with leaders and taught me a tremendous amount about them and their organizations that I couldn't have gotten any other way. Here are some specifics that I look for.

Leaders Listen

When we moved to Orlando, Florida, we asked a personal friend to put together a group of nonprofits who worked in the homelessness sector. We had learned so much from Jamie in Denver, and we were honestly excited to see what Orlando was doing. That day, we met several local leaders, but all of them had the same pitch and were only asking for program dollars. Program dollars are very important but they are not about fixing the root of the problem, but rather about addressing the immediate need. One leader completely stood out. He was listening to my questions to the other people. He was taking notes. When it was his turn to present, he addressed personally every question that I had had for the other nonprofits. He had taken the time to hear what I was asking, and he knew that I didn't want to fund program dollars. We wanted to invest in a program that would transform the old system, making access more efficient, and for more people. This leader got it.

Leaders Communicate Clearly and Often

First and most important, a great leader is a great communicator. Whenever I meet people for the first time, I always ask them to give me their elevator speech on their organization, their program, or themselves. I can quickly tell what kind of a leader the person is by what they are saying. Leaders who understand their challenges, know their goals, and know how to communicate them effectively are leaders worth backing. Look for leaders who have something important to say and who say it well.

No matter how busy leaders are, if they care about you and your donations, they will respond right away, even if it is just to tell you they can't get to your request for a day or so. They always acknowledge your comments, concerns, or questions. Given our plugged-in society of today, even nonprofits get messages on their smartphones. There is no excuse for lack of communication.

Leaders Think Outside the Box

Dave Krepcho is president and CEO of Second Harvest Food Bank of Central Florida, a member of Feeding America. Dave had been helping get food to the needy for more than twenty years. Before that, he was in the advertising business, where he honed his powers of persuasion. His proposal to us was simple but brilliant, a classic example of tracing a problem to its root, then thinking outside the box to come up with a solution.

Dave explained to us that the state offices where people applied for food stamps were typically not located near bus lines, making it hard for people to get to the office to apply. Instead, the average person had to take the entire day off of work (65 percent of food stamp recipients have a job[17]) and ride two, three, or four buses to the state office to apply. Once they waited in line for two or three hours, if they were approved, they would then have to wait weeks for the final approval via mail and then have to do a phone interview.

Dave's proposal was a three-year pilot program to fund five new jobs. This innovative pilot funded positions that they designated as their field outreach specialists. These specialists would have a fast track and immediate access to the state office. Instead of a person going through the earlier steps, individuals could apply online with the specialist. Part of the grant from us put laptop computers, cell phones, and portable fax machines right in the specialists' cars for immediate access. Dave negotiated a dedicated line to the state office, where the fax would be received, the family verified, and the benefits turned on. This was a transformative grant we couldn't resist. We could help people in need get back on their feet, especially families with children (47 percent of food stamp recipients are children; one out of four is under the age of five).[18]

We approved the three-year pilot program with Second Harvest. Within a few weeks, once the specialists had been hired and trained, Dave was emailing us with some of the most heart-warming and heart-wrenching stories we had ever heard. One of my favorites is about a family of seven. The mom and dad had recently become sick and had medical challenges, and their cupboards were bare. The five kids took turns going to school because they only had one pair of shoes. Each child took a turn going to school by the rotation of the shoes. The specialists got them signed up for food stamps immediately. Fortunately, Dave is also a great partner with Publix Super Markets, and they equip the field specialists with $10 gift cards that can be used immediately. Thanks to the specialist's training, a quick call to United Way got the children their shoes that they so desperately needed so that all of them could attend school at once, not just on rotation. (Here's another case where small gifts make a huge difference. The $10 gift card was just as important to this family that day as the on-site specialist. On other grants, John and I are often the $10 donor. We get just as much joy from both sizes of grants, because we know that the families in need are getting help.)

Leaders Leverage Gifts

Dave's brilliant idea illustrates a number of key characteristics of leaders. By coming up with the concept of specialists, Dave cut through a whole list of difficulties—lack of transportation, confusing application processes, poor literacy skills—with a single solution. On top of that, he leveraged donations to Second Harvest Food Bank with government funds that were available for the asking and would have otherwise either gone elsewhere or gone to waste. Good leaders know how to leverage a gift to make it go further.

Dave identified a gap where families that really needed food would never have signed up for food stamps without help from the field specialists. Without Dave's understanding of his community, hundreds of families would remain hungry today. In the first year of this program, the new team of specialists signed up families for the federally supported Supplemental Nutritional Assistance Program (SNAP—the official name for food stamps) totaling *$10 million in aid.*

I don't think when we approved this grant that any of us really understood the need of the Orlando community, or that the only way to successfully help our neighbors was to leverage the SNAP program. Our investment in the specialists earned a 4,000 percent return on investment *in our first year*! Again, this put $10 million in SNAP benefits into the Orlando community. Second Harvest has become the top nonprofit qualifier for federal food dollars in the country. Dave and his team of five specialists have become national role models for the SNAP program, training many other cities in how to replicate their success.

Leaders Are Not Quick to Judge

On a site visit, Dave shared with me what happened while helping to hand out food, "When I was observing a food distribution, a Cadillac Escalade (yes, the classic story you hear) drove up to receive food. My mind immediately went into stereotype mode . . . *Why is this lady taking food? She obviously does not need it.* My food bank spirit sank." The agency volunteer went to the open window of the Escalade and asked the lady how she could be helped. She replied, "I brought Agnes, a member of my church, to get some food. I've driven by before and observed what you do. Agnes is elderly, her husband is disabled, they don't have a car, and they need food."

Being the good communicator that Dave is, he shared this story in the *Orlando Sentinel*. Here is part of the response he received back:

> *Thank you for the reminder to all of us not to rush to judge others. My husband lost his job with a company where he had worked for thirty-seven years. Since that*

occurred in 2009, he has been laid off from five jobs. He is currently working outside of his field—part time— and making less than half what he had been making.

Thankfully we were frugal over the years and have had enough reserve to pay our bills and put food on the table. We also have a home for which we are thankful.

I often think about how people perceive us on the outside. Do they assume we're not struggling because my husband worked for a well-known company for so many years? Most of our friends think we are happy—unaffected by our trials. They don't see the pain we're hiding underneath our smiles. I think that is probably true for a lot of others as well. It all goes back to that stereotype mode you spoke of.

Thank you for your sensitivity to individual needs and for the reminder to "take time to consider what's really happening." May we all strive to enable others when we can.

Leaders Make You Feel Like Part of the Team

From the beginning of our relationship, Dave stayed in close contact with us, and his email let us share in the success of the field specialists program and all the other good work that Second Harvest Food Bank does. Dave also shared with us what he calls "thirty-second updates." When there was a special story, like the one quoted previously, we would get a one-way communication from Dave. No need to respond—he was just keeping us in the loop. This was very powerful for me, because I felt like I was part of the work being done to help families even though it wasn't me doing the work. Dave and his team made me feel like part of the organization. We have used this idea as an example for other causes. I cannot stress how important it is that the leaders you invest in make you feel like part of their good work.

If you are a nonprofit leader and you are reading this book, don't wait for the annual report to tell us what you did. That is 364 days away from the time you got the grant. Take Dave's model and develop your own type of one-way communication keeping your donor in the loop.

Dave Krepcho leads this dynamic team in providing food to the hungry in Orlando through Second Harvest Food Bank.

Leaders Find Gaps and Fill Them

Another leadership quality that Dave has is the ability to make changes in his operations and objectives to fit changes in the needs of the people he serves. He saw a need to advance from collecting food and signing up the needy for SNAP to providing a better place to house his organization. When Second Harvest

Food Bank of Orlando decided to build a new headquarters, Dave spearheaded the design of a facility that became a new national standard for food banks—improving efficiency and reducing waste. In the center of the building he put a community kitchen and culinary teaching facility. There is a need for people to be trained for good jobs. Answering that need while sticking to their mission, Second Harvest created a teaching kitchen. There is a classroom where tutors can help some of the students prepare for their GED while also teaching vital life skills. At the kitchen they train adult learners for jobs in the cooking and catering industries. Up to fifteen trainees at a time take their sixteen-week cooking course. Of the nine people who took their first class in 2013, seven of them immediately found jobs. Second Harvest is not only feeding America, it's also cooking for America and training new chefs! Great leaders identify gaps in their communities and fill them.

Leaders Know Their Business from the Bottom Up

The best leaders know their business from the bottom up. They may have been on the management fast track, but they realize they can't be effective unless they understand how the whole organization works. They also have to know their customers. This is *especially* true in the case of nonprofits, where the "customers" tend to be people on the margins of the community, often without a voice, and seldom understood by the people who are supposedly there to help them.

Dave tackled the issue of knowing his "customers" and understanding their needs and challenges by spending some time living like they live. He and his wife lived for a week on what a couple in Orlando gets from SNAP—$86! This worked out to about $2 per meal. After the experience, Dave had a new appreciation for what it's like to go to the grocery and have to watch every cent; to worry about getting to the checkout and not having enough money; the struggle to eat healthy when the cheap choices are packed with salt and carbohydrates; having to skip the allergy medicine that would have eaten up a quarter of their budget. Even then, as he noted in his blog about the experience, he still had advantages. "We are a household with a car," he wrote. "Forty percent of SNAP households do not have access to their own transportation." To get through the week they had to put less ground beef in the chili. They had to buy fewer tomatoes and slice them thinner.

And there was the stigma of being poor, if only for a week. "As we discussed our choices, my wife became aware that people might overhear and think we were poor. We actually lowered our voices." Shopping for variety? Having friends over for dinner? Indulging in an occasional martini? Out of the question. Once he had this experience, Dave saw his job in an entirely new light. If you find a leader with insights on this level, you'll find a leader worth investing in.

Leaders Take Care of Their Workers

Leaders need to look out for the little things that make their workers' jobs easier. They need to walk the halls and be aware of things like silly bureaucracy and elevators that don't work and lunch rooms that are not maintained. You'd be surprised at the amount of goodwill you can create by keeping an eye out for those sorts of things. General Eisenhower called it being sure your soldiers had dry socks.

Leaders Speak Out

To make changes in the system, great leaders speak out. Their voice can be their most powerful tool, representing hundreds or thousands of voices that might not be heard otherwise.

Mistakes Are Okay

In the process of identifying leaders, you have to make some educated guesses. True leaders prove themselves over time, and it usually isn't clear or obvious for a while whether your pick was a good one or not. If you do it right, you will take some chances. Not all leaders act like Dave. Sometimes you will make mistakes. We do. Don't let this bother you too much. As my father-in-law tells me, "If we aren't making mistakes, we're not taking enough risks." Learn from your mistakes and move on. Mistakes aren't a sign of failure; they're a sign of growth and learning.

Think about your mistake, what did you learn from the experience, and how will you be better next time? Lessons learned in these situations are sometimes more valuable than success.

In a recent funding mistake that I made, not only was I out a ton of personal time, but also our foundation contributed $75,000 that didn't have the impact we expected. As I evaluated what went wrong, I compared that money to what we could have invested in with Dave. Based on his track record, he could have added three more specialists to his program for SNAP, touched thousands of people, and brought in another $3.6 million in federal assistance.

Great leaders aren't always easy to find, but they're always worth looking for and supporting. They become extensions of your arms, legs, and brain, multiplying the work you're able to accomplish. Once they've proven their value, encourage them, compliment them, and reward them. The more they can share in the satisfaction of a job well done, the more eager they'll be to join you in climbing the next mountain.

Chapter 9

Clone Your Cash

C onsider two possible scenarios for the next donation you make. In the first, the grateful recipient accepts your check and spends it on something the organization needs. In the second, the grateful recipient accepts your check, finds a source of matching funds to double the value of your gift, negotiates a deep discount on items they buy, and ends up getting $3 worth of value for every dollar you invested. A top criterion of mine when I consider a donation is how far the organization can stretch the money I give. When you're doing research on nonprofits to support, look carefully at how well they multiply the value of your contribution. Don't invest $100 in one place when another one can turn that $100 into $200 or $300 in buying power.

For example, many United Way agencies qualify for federal government matching funds. If you give them $100, the government matches it with another hundred. There are lots of sources for these matching funds that can leverage your gift in incredible ways, including local city bonds and a long list of state and federal programs. In many cases, the charity has to raise money first to qualify for these matching funds. This creates a huge motivation on their part to partner with you in order to pull down these additional dollars. When that happens, they get your donation plus the matching funds, and you get the satisfaction of seeing your gift leveraged to a higher value.

Matching funds turn a modest gift into a bigger one. So do small, steady donations that accumulate over time. Say you want to contribute to a building program at your church. You'd like to give at a certain level but you have to work within your budget. You set aside $200 a month for the project and give that much regularly, year after year. After ten years—not that long in the life of a church—your donation has grown to $24,000!

I'm always on the lookout for grantees that make the most of matching funds and who are grateful for my donations even when they start small. My husband and I began partnering with our local Mile High United Way years ago because of the opportunity to leverage the amount we donated through matching funds. Better yet, much of these additional donations brought in even more in matching dollars through a pull down from the federal government, and 100 percent of it would be going toward early childhood education. Without granting a single dollar directly to early childhood development for Colorado, our match was pulling down $2 million per year for the cause. Yet even this wasn't good enough for Mile High United Way president and CEO Christine Benero. She knew she could make our money grow even more. She turned enthusiastically to the business community, asking them to match our $2 million and the federal $2 million together. Her perseverance won the day. Christine and the staff at Mile High United Way turned our $2 million gift into $8 million for the Denver community.

Whatever amount you decided to donate, imagine the satisfaction of knowing that every $2 you put in had the buying power of $8! It's like cloning your cash. That's the kind of nonprofit that deserves your support.

Another way to multiply the value of your gift is to create a tipping point. This is the moment when you and others have put enough behind an organization or idea for it to achieve critical mass: suddenly it has forward momentum and everybody wants to invest and get involved.

A few years ago at a lunch in Aspen, I met a sweet man named David Wick from KIPP—Knowledge Is Power Program—which runs charter schools all across the country. KIPP was founded in 1994 by two teachers—Dave Levin and Mike Feinberg—with one school in Houston. At the time David Wick and I met, KIPP had about 125 schools running in fifteen or so regions or large cities. The results they achieved were phenomenal, sometimes showing a double-digit increase in standardized test scores compared to a public school that might be just across the street. Same students, same community, and a completely different motto: "Work Hard, Be Nice!" Today there are about sixty thousand KIPP students and alumni, each getting a fantastic education that prepares them for success in the future.

David and I really hit it off. I was impressed by his enthusiasm and dedication. We found common ground in our passion for education and our belief that, in general, the public schools in America have really let down our low-income students, especially minorities. I was surprised to learn that KIPP had done what it had so far with little or no technology. Imagine what they could do if they had state-of-the-art teaching tools!

Later that day, my friend Dr. Michael Salem and I were planning a hike on the Ute Trail near my house, and I asked David to join us. I often invite new friends for a hike or a bike ride. It helps me clear my head and make room for fresh thinking. It also shows the other person some of what's important to me: good health, the outdoors, and respecting the environment. Michael is president and CEO of National Jewish Health in Denver, which our foundation has supported with several large gifts over the years. As we walked, Michael told David about the impact our foundation has had on a school for medically frail students at his hospital. He went on to describe how engaged the students were, how the teachers were all trained to use technology, and that this year each child would be learning on their own laptop, at their own pace, getting exactly what they needed to fill the gaps caused by missing so much school due to illness. The common ground here is the students attending school at National Jewish Health come in years behind their grade level, just like some of the KIPP kids.

Two KIPP students engaged in learning with their new technology. Work Hard, Be Nice.

I know that the confidence and experience Dr. Salem shared with David gave me credibility that I couldn't have gotten anywhere else. David was eager to talk with us about a possible gift to KIPP. There were a couple of times I thought he wasn't going to make it to the end of the hike (we were at 9,000 feet), but he was so excited about the prospect of a partnership with us that he hung in there until the end.

I now had three vital components I needed to make a difference. First, I had an idea: bring technology into the classroom for KIPP, much like we did for National Jewish Health. Second, I had the means: a grant from our foundation. Third, I was getting the credibility I needed from Michael Salem's talk with David. Unless I had that credibility, no nonprofit would pay attention to my recommendations. Of course they'd take my money, but I wanted to do more than write a check.

They knew more about what was needed and how to implement it than I did; we had to be good listeners if our grant to KIPP would be a success. KIPP made the process simple because unlike so many schools, theirs isn't a top-down organization. The teachers and principals have a lot of power to make decisions and delegate resources. All KIPP principals were invited to apply. Only the principals who saw the power of technology in the classroom applied. The rest did not.

At the foundation we had lots of experience rolling out Requests for Proposals. This time, talking with David Wick and others, we came up with the idea of a Request for Collaboration. What did they need? How could we work together beyond the point of handing over a donation to help them move ahead? We wanted to invite individual schools to apply for money to bring technology to their classrooms. To get their attention we decided to start with a big gift of $750,000. To our amazement, our grant offer brought in requests for more than $3 million from the KIPP network of schools.

How could we decide which programs to fund and which to reject? The KIPP team knew the answer to that far better than we did. We formed a grants committee with five members from KIPP and two from our foundation. We collected all the requests, got together on a conference call, and in four hours had made all the decisions. Some schools got everything they asked for, some got part, and some got no grant at all.

Our gift drew attention to the power of technology as a teaching tool. Once they had the opportunity to add it to their classrooms, teachers suddenly saw what an incredible advantage it gave their kids. We had begun to reach a tipping point: more schools in the KIPP network wanted technology. The first year we'd looked at $3 million in grant requests. By the second year the results had proved how much high-tech teaching could help KIPP. We received grant requests for the second round of funding that topped $8 million! This was more than double the demand of year one.

By year three, more than half of KIPP schools were demanding technology in the classroom and we continued our investment. With almost sixty thousand students standing to benefit from our involvement, and with the KIPP leadership making every dollar we spent do the work of three or four, it has been more than fulfilling to partner with them.

———•———

Another project where leverage, as well as teamwork, played a huge part was our collaboration with the Denver Museum of

Nature and Science. An energetic and dedicated man named George Sparks heads the organization and asked us for a major contribution to their capital campaign for a new building. The city had issued bonds to cover half the cost, and he knew of several possible sources for additional funds, including the Morgridge Family Foundation. What he needed was someone to take the lead: just like the penguin that is the first to jump in the water, we were the first donors to inspire others to follow.

Dr. Bridget Coughlin with early learners at the Denver Museum of Nature and Science, Discovery Zone.

The price tag for the whole project was far more than our budget would allow. However, we knew that if we could inspire others to give, our gift and their contributions—along with the public funds from the bonds—would get the job done. (Every gift to the museum also benefits from the leverage of three thousand volunteers who serve there every year, saving $3 million in annual operating expenses.) Something I've witnessed firsthand is that giving is contagious. In fact, a study (by James Fowler of the University of California, San Diego and Nicholas Christakis of Harvard) published in the *Proceedings of the National Academy of Science*[9] confirms this. So, we agreed to grant the museum $8 million (about 11 percent of the total.) That got the ball rolling. Today the new museum welcomes 1.2 million visitors a year, more than the Denver Broncos and Colorado Rockies teams attendance combined. With the new facility, the number of little visitors (ages birth to five) has skyrocketed from seventeen thousand a month to fifty thousand.

You can probably think of giving goals you'd like to reach that are far beyond what you can do alone. We couldn't have built a museum, but we could challenge and inspire others by donating a gift of our own with the hope that they would join us in building for the future. That's exactly what happened. By leveraging your resources and working as a team you will be amazed at what you can achieve.

Chapter 10

Outside the Box

Einstein defined insanity as doing the same thing over and over and expecting different results. Yes, this seems like a no-brainer. It shouldn't take a certified genius to tell us that if one plan of action fails to work we should do something else, even if it seems radical at the time. But we're all creatures of habit. We love the familiar; we're at ease with the tried and true. When you get into a comfortable routine, it's tempting to stick with it and hope the situation will improve. But when you fail to get the results you want, the time comes when you have to step outside your comfort zone and try something different. You have to think outside the box. Sometimes the best, most successful ideas come completely out of left field. Don't be afraid of them. Welcome them.

There are two aspects to consider here. First, as a donor to worthy causes, you have to be willing to think outside the box. Second, you have to keep a constant watch for prospective grantees or organizations who think outside the box. It could be an idea only a few steps away from the predictable that breaks up a frustrating logjam. Or it might be a crazy notion that knocks your socks off on its way to innovation and success.

I do a lot of thinking while riding my mountain bike, swimming, or running. There's something about the process of pushing myself physically that clears my brain and helps me think in new directions. Those are the times when I think outside the box and look for examples of other people who do the same.

Searching for answers in unlikely places is always interesting, and sometimes revolutionary. Author and *New Yorker* writer Malcolm Gladwell couldn't figure out why, after a lifetime as a law-abiding citizen, he was suddenly getting speeding tickets, being pulled over for interrogation in airport security lines, and stopped by police in the street. The reason, it turned out, was his long, curly hair. It was similar to the hair of a criminal at large, even though in all other features Gladwell and the criminal looked nothing alike. The situation prompted Gladwell to think about how people make decisions quickly based on past experiences and information. He published his study as *Blink: The Power of Thinking Without Thinking* (New York: Little, Brown, 2005), which became one of the most honored books of the decade, selling more than two million copies. In fact, all of Gladwell's books tell us something about the way we think and the way we succeed—all by looking outside the box of conventional behavioral science.

One of the greatest outside-the-box thinkers of our time began with the idea that computers ought to be available to everybody. Back in the 1970s, computers were big, expensive machines that spoke some alien language like FORTRAN or A-Basic, took up a whole room, and worked by processing big reels of magnetic tape or infuriating stacks of paper punch cards. Steve Jobs didn't do market research or study the business plans of the established computer companies. He took a radical jump outside the box to develop a comparatively tiny, simple computer called the Macintosh that sat on a desk, took commands in plain English, and soon revolutionized the world we live in.

The potential of thinking outside the box is unlimited, yet the initial barriers to it can be tough to break down. One reason is inertia. Changing directions is harder than strolling on down the same path. You have to decide that overcoming inertia is worth the trouble. Another reason stepping outside the box is hard is that you naturally wonder what other people will think. Is your idea so odd or radical that people you know will be critical? You have to believe in your new direction enough to take some kidding or criticism from friends who are convinced they know better. A third challenge is fear of failure. What if it all blows up in your face? Well at least you tried something, rather than sticking with a plan that doesn't work and remaining a member of the Einstein Insanity Club. A fourth obstacle is the general fear we all have of the unknown. Maybe we're born with it—afraid of the dark and strange noises—but regardless, it has a grip on us when we try to venture into new territory.

Philanthropy can be an adventure. Of course you have to do your research, but part of the reward of giving is to use your imagination to come up with ways to do things better. Remember, the first rule of philanthropy is supporting a cause you're passionate about. If you believe in the objective, looking for fresh ways to achieve it will be fun.

Outside the Box for Foster Care

I've mentioned my work in the foster care system. Colorado has over six thousand young people in foster care.[20] Every year over five hundred of them turn eighteen and no longer qualify for services within the child welfare system.[21] Within six months, half of them will be homeless. These young people had been forgotten until Mile High United Way stepped in with their program, Bridging the Gap.

This program has drastically changed the quality of life for many young people and put them in positions where they can be successful adults. Take Paul for instance, a twenty-year-old man who had been on the streets of Denver for two years. Now, thanks to Bridging the Gap, he has a safe place to live; an internship at a construction company; is earning his GED online; and has testified in front of the state legislature, the Department of Human Services, and other child welfare organizations—giving a voice to the young people that don't have the chance to explain their situations to the people who are making the decisions that affect their lives. But the true story here is that Bridging the Gap was a new approach that can change the lives of every young person in the Colorado child welfare system.

As I have shared with you previously, Mile High United Way invested in a collaboration between the Colorado Department of Health and Human Services and the Colorado Department of Education. The objective was to research and understand how these two very different (and sometimes isolated) departments and their respective policies affected the people they were committed to serving. An evaluative research project produced data that had never been seen before. The results were so startling to policymakers and administrative staff that these two separate state agencies have jointly funded a position to continue this work and break down barriers that will allow Paul and hundreds of other young people to thrive.

This type of administrative teamwork might not have the

emotional appeal that some investors are seeking, but it is innovative thinking that will change everything for a young person who has been forgotten. Frances Wisebart Jacobs, one of the founders of the United Way network, wrote: *"God never made a pauper in the world—children come into the world and conditions and surroundings make them either princes or paupers."*[22] Investments both big and small change these conditions and the surroundings for every one of us. They unite us, they give us hope, and they deliver results.

The people at Mile High United Way were willing to invest their time and talent to change the system. By continuing to do the same things in the same way, we were not realizing the human potential of the hundreds of kids exiting out of the foster care system. As a result of the pilot, these young people in the system now have a fighting chance.

Education for the Twenty-First Century

Visionary people are taking a new look at education. If we keep delivering the content in the same way, we will get the same results: student opportunity and performance will be uneven, and employers won't see the skills they need in new job seekers. I'm convinced that Salman Khan is one of the biggest education disruptors of our time. He thinks way, *way* outside the box. I wrote about him earlier, but he merits a mention here too as a great example of taking a well-worn process in an entirely new direction.

In 2003, Sal started posting math lessons on YouTube to help tutor his niece. He actually jokes that his niece preferred watching him on the videos than speaking to him on the phone. What Sal discovered was that his niece needed time to digest the material—to stop, rewind, and maybe even listen to the math concept again. In realizing this, he tapped into every teacher's dream of seeing their students learn on their own outside the classroom as well as in the school, and having fun no matter where the learning takes place.

Almost five years later, Sal quit his job and started developing and posting lessons full time. "I teach the way I wish I was taught," Sal explained, with lessons coming from "an actual human being who is fascinated by the world around him." Khan Academy has come a long way in just eight years. It's a platform of lessons and videos, which has had more than two billion problem questions solved. It's really delivering on its mission to provide a free world-class education for anyone anywhere.

Upon learning about Khan Academy from a partner school, we had to bring Sal out to Denver to speak at our Share Fair event. The first session was for teachers to learn about best practices, emergent strategies, and innovative approaches to delivering twenty-first century learning. The second, and public, component is called STEMosphere, a full day of fun and brains-on interactive activities, informational exhibits, creative competitions, and net-working among those with a vested interest in STEM, arts, and entrepreneurship. Sal was our first-ever keynote speaker at this event. His team flew with him to Denver and trained our Colorado teachers.

Immediately afterward, the Morgridge Family Foundation team visited Khan Academy. Sal gave us a tour of where he makes the videos. I delivered a short presentation to his staff on the focus of our foundation and the types of projects we fund. We knew there had to be a project we could collaborate on that would be the right fit for a Morgridge Family Foundation/Khan Academy partnership.

Carrie and John Morgridge hosting Sal Khan for Share Fair Nation held at the University of Denver.

After talking with teachers, students, and administrators who use Khan Academy, I can tell you they think it's fantastic. What they need, however, is access. To use Khan resources at school, students need a laptop or a tablet and access to the internet. Through our grants and a strong partnership with Khan Academy, we have trained hundreds of teachers and put thousands of devices directly into classrooms.

We're seeing that schools that have technology woven into the fabric of classroom teaching produce the highest gains. Yet as wonderful as these results are, technology is never going to replace a master teacher in the classroom. Parents, school boards, and superintendents who fear some huge educational machine taking control out of their hands have nothing to worry about. It's a matter of master teaching AND technology, not master teaching OR technology. Both are incredibly important to personalized learning.

The stack of heartfelt thank-you notes I get from teachers and students every week tells the story. A student in Pembroke, Massachusetts, wrote, "For homework we go on Khan Academy each night for twenty minutes. But we love it so most people do double of that! Khan Academy really helped me with things I didn't understand. Each day, I get smarter and smarter because of Khan Academy. I learn new things and new tricks of those new things. I will have an excellent math life."

A teacher sent this card: "With the switch to the Common Core State Standards in Louisiana, I'm finding myself charged with teaching skills I've never taught before. Although I've been teaching math for over four years, I go straight to Khan Academy to learn a skill myself . . . What I'd like to do is bridge the gap between my being able to access Khan Academy and my students, so they can get an even greater benefit. Although we have a wonderful amount of time together in class, more access to Khan in the school day will enable kids to grow in their lagging academic skills faster and more excitedly. Khan is fun!"

This teacher shared with her students the exact amount our foundation had donated to her class for technology. One of the kids wrote, "I think paying $1,500 was worth it! I do a lot of time on Khan Academy, so I mastered a lot of skills . . . It's like a school on a computer. Thank You!"

A teacher in Idaho shared her story with us: "I love how well Khan is matching up with Common Core State Standards, and I appreciate that it holds students accountable for learning material rather than just earning completion grades from traditional homework. The mastery challenges force students to retain the lessons over time versus just remembering concepts for a specific chapter. I honestly feel that this will revolutionize my instruction and dedication to student learning."

In the course of working with Khan Academy, I learned that it's one thing to ask a school if it has "technology" and quite another to probe a little deeper to see if their technology is modern enough to do any good! When we ask a school or district if they have technology in the classroom, they all answer yes. But a lot of them struggle with outdated systems that hold them back. As one teacher explained, "Our current laptops (eight years old) struggle utilizing Khan Academy. Although students are able to log on and use the site, the age of the laptops results in a lot of down time rebooting screen freezes, waiting for activities and videos to load, and several times a week students waste twenty minutes allotted for Khan Academy instruction because their laptop struggles to boot up and load the site properly."

Now instead of asking if a school has technology we ask, "Do you have what you need in your classroom to teach the way you want to teach? How many minutes a day are your students learning on a computer versus how many minutes would you like to see your students learning on a computer?" Simply changing this question for teachers who are applying for grants has helped us to become better donors.

If you share my passion for bringing technology into the classroom, it's something you can do on a very modest budget. Acer Chromebooks, which teachers love to use, are currently listed on the Walmart website for $199. The DonorsChoose.org website puts thousands of convenient giving opportunities at your fingertips. The last time I used the site, I entered my office zip code and got a list of 5,567 projects to fund in my own neighborhood.

On the DonorsChoose website one teacher had posted, "These days, a classroom without technology is like a warehouse without forklifts—no matter how stocked the shelves, how rich the wares, there isn't any good way to deliver the merchandise. My students are motivated. I'm working on transitioning my old-school classroom to a future-proof, high-tech house of learning. With a Chromebook—my classroom will be always connected."

He was requesting $125.25 that would complete his request for one laptop. I couldn't say no!

Ten Million Coders

Another disruptor who thinks outside the box in the world of education is someone whose name you might not know right off, but if you've learned to program online with the forty-plus million other people on code.org then you know Hadi Partovi. I met Hadi at the Jeb Bush annual conference, Foundation for Excellence in Education. Hadi was super impressive and was laser focused on his huge goal of teaching ten million students to code—meaning computer science coding—in a one-week period. I had to say I wasn't sure if this was even achievable, but Hadi assured me they would hit their goal.

During our conversation Hadi said, "STEM is a very hot education topic, and it should be. In the next twenty years most jobs will be in a STEM field." What I didn't understand then is that if you break down the STEM data, 90 percent of the STEM jobs are in computer science in some capacity. Yet computer science is seriously underrepresented in the K–12 environment.

A February 26, 2013, article in the *Huffington Post* quoted Hadi as saying, "At a time when most English majors graduate jobless, computer science majors are twice as likely to land a job. Computers are our job-creation engine, and programmers earn among the highest salaries in America. Ironically, computer education in K–12 has declined over the past decade. Fewer schools, fewer teachers, and fewer students engage in this field than ten years ago. Only nine states even recognize computer science as a math or science discipline! Only 10 percent of schools even offer it. This is easy to change, and it's time to start."[23]

Because most high schools don't even have a class code for computer science, step one was to convince districts around the county to add coding as a class. The next step for making computer science more accessible for all was to create free online content for both teachers and students, just like Khan Academy. I don't think you will be surprised to learn that besides Hadi investing in his own nonprofit, his big investors that helped get code.org launched were Bill Gates and Mark Zuckerberg.

I personally participated in the hour of code on the first day of the launch. I will admit it was super fun, and I just wanted to get that bird! There were hands-on instructions directing the user to code sequence winding through a maze to get a bird. The last sequence was challenging for me, but maybe not for you and definitely not hard for students who are barely half my size. After completing my hour of code, I immediately got a certificate, which I proudly printed out and hung in my office.

So how did code.org do toward reaching their lofty goal? They made it. More than ten million students participated. There were so many partners during the week that Apple stores had coding sections, libraries had extended hours, and schools focused for the day and the week, making sure that every student had an opportunity to code. I heard from a teacher friend in Florida who had a student who couldn't read very well. Once the student started mastering the codes and learning the next step, a light bulb went on. He could do it! Coding was fun, he was good at it, and for the first time this student had a success at school.

By August 2014, just eight months after the original launch, Hadi told us, "We've introduced forty million students to an Hour of Code; we've put online computer science courses into thirty-one thousand classrooms in under eight months with 40 percent [of the students being] girls. We've trained seven hundred teachers for classes starting this fall paying them stipends, and we'll be training six thousand to ten thousand more during this school year. We've changed policies in fourteen states, with two of the largest (CA and NY) on deck to change policy by the end of the summer."

These two examples are big projects, but they all started as a simple idea—a way to do a familiar task and meet a familiar challenge in a new way. Don't be afraid to think big. There's no telling what sort of support your idea might attract, or what kind of revolution you might start right in your own living room. That's what thinking outside the box is all about.

Chapter 11

Unintended Consequences

One of the best rewards of giving is when you help someone you didn't even start out to help. You donate to a cause you're passionate about, and then realize your gift has the unintended consequences of helping somebody else too; or there's an extra, unexpected benefit for the people you donate to. This is part of the joy of giving. And if the extra benefits are in other areas you're also passionate about, you've hit a philanthropic home run.

The Amazing Dr. Goodall

When our office received a call from a partner in Denver asking if we might be able to pull together a handful of teachers to have dinner with Dr. Jane Goodall, we jumped at the chance. What a great way to thank teachers—by inviting them to a private dinner with Goodall, known around the world for her lifelong study of African chimpanzees and her tireless support of conservation. At the dinner she spoke about the importance of youth and about her program Roots and Shoots sponsored by the Jane Goodall Institute. The program teaches children to map their own communities, identify environmental gaps, and find solutions for closing them. From a start with a dozen students on Dr. Goodall's porch in Africa, Roots and Shoots has grown to 150,000 members in more than 130 countries.[24]

Carrie Morgridge shares the stage with Dr. Jane Goodall to kick off Share Fair Nation in Denver before 5,000 teachers, students, and families.

Judging by the incredible reception Dr. Goodall received at the dinner, it was clear to us that she should be the keynote speaker at our next Share Fair Nation event. To our surprise and delight, she accepted. We took advantage of every minute, scheduling her at a frantic pace, but she was unfailingly gracious about it. We booked her for a teacher event at the Denver Museum of Nature and Science, a private dinner, a public speech at the University of Denver, and more. Despite her eighty years, this woman kept an impressive pace.

At the teacher dinner, Jane told me she wanted to have some fun. She and Sanjayan, her colleague at The Nature Conservancy, went to the front of the room to give a speech. Instead of starting with their remarks, they both acted like chimpanzees, scratching each other's heads and sounding the mating call. The crowd roared—then we all took our turn scratching our heads and calling out! Jane then had the entire room hold hands with those nearest them while she shared her beliefs about how much people need to have connections with and love for others and how each one of us plays an important role in loving and caring for others in this world.

The next morning she drew a full audience at the University of Denver Magness Arena. The crowd was mesmerized by Jane's story of her childhood curiosity about where an egg came from. You could have heard a pin drop as she described following a chicken into the hen house and waiting for an egg to appear.

Unexpectedly, Dr. Goodall introduced us to her lifelong friends in Denver, Jon and Renee Zahourek, founders of Anatomy in Clay. They created and developed a learning system to demonstrate the anatomy of muscles for drawing classes at the Parsons School of Design in New York. As Jon explained, "Our goal is to empower self-discovery in each of us by forming anatomy with our own hands." The non-tech, hands-on process that takes place when people play with clay is fascinating. Because Jane recommended them so highly, we jumped at the chance to invite them to teach at our Share Fair STEMosphere event.

Later that day when my husband John was at the Anatomy in Clay booth, a man came up to him almost in tears. His daughter, who had severe autism, had never sat still more than three seconds for most of her life. When she discovered Anatomy in Clay, she sat for four hours, rolling each muscle out of clay, and looking back and forth between her arm and the displayed clay muscles. I remember this grateful dad thanking John for opening up the teacher event to the public. And it all happened because Jane Goodall wanted us to meet her Denver friends—unintended consequences that produced a small miracle one family will never forget.

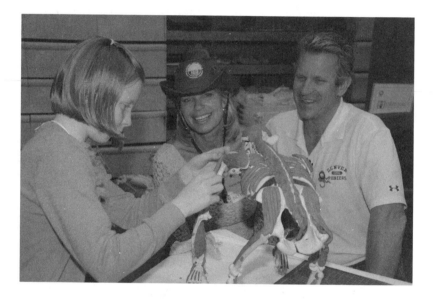

Student at STEMopshere working hard on her chimpanzee, teaching John and Carrie Morgridge about the muscles.

Horses to the Rescue

The area of Colorado where John and I live part of the year is horse country—not the rugged Rocky Mountains most people associate with our state, but beautiful rolling hills. Though our passion in philanthropy is mainly focused on education, we also love animals. Since the day we met, John and I have had a pet. So I was very interested in meeting Kathy Hamm and learning about Dream Catcher Therapy Center, which helps both kids and horses by bringing them together. I found out about Kathy from my mom, Val, a pediatric nurse near Telluride. Some of the pediatricians Mom works with send abused children to Dream Catcher Therapy to help them recover from their abuse and rebuild their lives.

This ranch rescues old horses through its End of Trail Horse Rescue and uses them in an equine rehabilitation center for children. They've also started a treatment program for returning military veterans with posttraumatic stress disorder.

Anything that involves children, veterans, and horses, count us in! We started with a grant of $1,500, enough to support three rescue horses for one year including food, shelter, and veterinary services. Though our initial aim was to help the horses, the unintended consequence was that the horses in turn provided therapy for children in need.

At one point Kathy asked me if I would donate a coffee pot to the veterans' lounge. She seemed a little embarrassed to make the request but I was thrilled to know of something specific I could do. While I was at it, I donated another $3,000 to give them a remodeled room for returning veterans to go with their coffee pot.

The more I knew about Kathy and the people at Dream Catcher Therapy, the more I wanted to help. During the recession that began in 2008 a lot of horse owners in the area started having trouble keeping up with expenses. An average horse eats about twenty pounds of hay a day and needs other care as well. Many owners needed help with feeding; a few even made the tough decision to give their animals away. Kathy had already been taking in abused and abandoned horses for years when she learned that a state-of-the-art horse facility was for sale nearby. It would, as Kathy wrote to me, "allow us to significantly expand our animal assisted therapy program, veterans program, and hay bank services, as well as provide the absolute best of care and rehabilitation for our neglected and abused, unwanted rescue horses." Because of our success in the past with Kathy, the Morgridge Family Foundation was eager to help fund the new facility.

We have photos in our office of the three horses we supported directly. When Kathy called to tell me that April, our original rescue horse, had passed, I will tell you that I cried. Kathy had done such a great job with April, and April had been giving therapy services to both children and veterans. I still get all choked up thinking about the work that Kathy does for horses and people alike.

Two rescue horses who are now well-fed and help both abused children and returning veterans thanks to the care of Dream Catcher Therapy.

Kathy went on to say, "When people and organizations make the time and effort to donate to our organization they are helping in ways they can never imagine. Every little bit, be it time or money, makes a huge difference to our clients and four-legged therapists. Many people ask us, 'Why a horse and not a dog?' How I respond is, 'Dogs buffer our emotions while horses mirror them back to us. That is why horses make us change something while dogs make us feel better.'" She also noted, "Our facility has witnessed for over a decade the healing impact that horses have on individuals with mental and physical challenges. It only seemed natural for us to provide a place of healing and sanctuary for our four-legged therapists. Watching a horse and a child or a veteran, both from environments filled with trauma, neither in control, leaning on each other to rebuild broken dreams, trust, and love is truly awe-inspiring. Changing the life of one animal might not make a huge difference in the world, but it means the world to that animal. I think that is why all of us are here [at Dream Catcher] today."

Kathy makes her donors feel like part of the healing process too. The more we knew about Dream Catcher Therapy Center and End of Trail Horse Rescue, the more we were committed to helping. You should feel so good about your gift to an organization like Kathy's that it becomes easy to give again and again.

The Power of Volunteers

On a flight home from two site visits in the Boston area, I ended up sitting next to an executive-looking man. We were both working away on our technology devices until the flight attendant instructed us to put our devices into airplane mode. I then dove into the stack of documents I had waiting to be read. My seatmate and I eventually picked up a casual conversation. David Campbell is a retired technology executive who ended up knowing my father-in-law. They had both been in the technology sector of business at the same time, though working for different companies.

David shared with me that since retiring he had discovered a new passion for volunteering in times of crisis. He said that when the tsunami hit Thailand in 2004 he watched the television coverage. The thing that caught his attention was that two of the three hotels there had been destroyed. The one remaining hotel informed the TV crew and media that they still had Internet. The Internet was David's business. Ten days later he flew to Phuket, Thailand, to help those in the disaster area stay connected with the rest of the world. He and some friends spent their own money to appeal online for volunteers to join them. A new term David had never heard of before, SUV—spontaneous unaffiliated volunteers—started to show up.

In the two weeks David was in Thailand eighty people from around the world came to volunteer. One of them said it was the most rewarding time of his life, and if David helped out during another disaster, he could count on this person. When Hurricane Katrina hit in the United States in 2005, David deployed in the same way. This is when David Campbell decided to create the All Hands Volunteers nonprofit. When a church in Mississippi offered to put up the Katrina volunteers, he thought about fifty would answer the call. Within a week 216 people had come to help, and they were all living in the church together.

I asked David if there was a special time, person, or place that became his "ah-ha moment." He said it was when they went to the Philippines and a digital photo restoration specialist was among the many volunteers. "It never dawned on me that this service would be needed," he said. "Families had lost everything, their businesses, their homes, their pets, and their families. When their volunteer saw the hundreds of treasured photos badly damaged she asked us to purchase some needed equipment, then scanned and retouched photos, eventually getting help from other experts all around the world."

"A couple showed up at the All Hands Volunteers base with a damaged photo. It was the only thing they had left of their daughter. Our volunteer was able to restore the photo and give it back to the couple, as the last physical reminder of their daughter." When this story hit the Web, dozens of other digital restoration experts went to work, and hundreds of additional photos were recovered. This is such a great example of giving with your own passion. I am assuming that the restoration photographer was not as excited to go live at a disaster zone; however, her passion made a forever-lasting effect on a family. The volunteers we have met through the All Hands Volunteers organization have brought their passion to rebuild with them, no matter where in the world God takes them.

David went to help rebuild the Philippines and found himself rebuilding lives.

Planting Seeds of Appreciation

A school garden is a space that can educate and inspire. The committed and driven teachers who use these spaces to help develop our next generations are incredible people. But perhaps even more incredible than the teachers are the students who love to garden and care for these spaces.

School gardens in urban areas often give youth a beautiful and safe place to relax from the many demands they face—often troubled home lives, dire economic circumstances, peer pressure, and random violence. The benefits from learning, playing, and engaging outdoors are many, including an increased understanding of science and the value of nature. But perhaps the most important effect that a school garden can have on children is its ability to cultivate their sense of self-efficacy and responsibility to their peers and communities.

This idea is put into action at Cross Country Elementary Middle School in Baltimore, Maryland. After receiving support from The Nature Conservancy to build an urban school garden, students worked together with teachers, volunteers, and community members to design and build a garden on their school campus. Their involvement from the very beginning in every step of the process has created a deep sense of responsibility on the part of the students to make sure "their garden" is healthy and thriving.

One afternoon after the garden was finished, a student and his much older brother walked through. Despite many protests from the student, the older brother vandalized several picnic tables in the space. Devastated that his garden had been harmed, the boy went home and convinced his father, a carpenter, to go to the school overnight and fix all the picnic tables so that by morning there was no evidence of any damage.

This simple story illustrates how a sense of ownership and responsibility on the part of one individual can have a ripple effect. Not only did this conscientious student restore the garden for his fellow classmates and teachers, but he also made sure that the space remained a beautiful and safe place for his community. His one act affected his entire class, school, and neighborhood and shows us that the seeds of community and environmental stewardship are sown in small acts.

On your journey of giving back to your own community, be open to the pleasant surprise of unintended consequences.

Someone you never met or even thought of may be harvesting the benefit of your generosity. The two of you likely will never meet, yet the power of your gift joins you together in a partnership of sharing and mutual respect.

Chapter 12

Filling the Gap

Montrose, Colorado, is a small town just outside the famous ski resort of Telluride. My mom works there as a pediatric nurse where, she says, "We can see the flu coming from Denver." They always get a wave of sick kids about a week after a flu bug hits the big city.

Beautiful as it is, the community has its share of people who fall on hard times. They just need a slight lift up or guidance on where to look for help. And while there's a variety of public and private assistance available for these residents, there always seems to be a gap that leaves families without essential services or that little boost to get them through a tough situation. Dr. Mary Vader has made it her business to step in and fill that gap.

Dr. Vader is one of the doctors in the office where Mom works. She has become a friend and inspiration to my mom and a good friend to me as well. Her work in Montrose is a great example of another kind of giving that's less structured than the usual methods, but that can be just as powerful. It meets needs that may not be met any other way. The gifts are usually relatively small (once again, small gifts can do the most good!), immediate, and they cut through bureaucratic procedures to satisfy the need quickly and simply.

Dr. Vader was the seventh of eleven children born to a ranching family in Gunnison. Her career as a doctor is a natural result of her lifelong compassion for others. She also studied for the nondenominational ministry in order to be a hospital chaplain and perform weddings. She says, "I don't preach, but I do try to follow the teachings of Christ and try to be a good role model for my patients and their families. Yes, I still cuss. I try to teach others that there is a consequence for every action, and that the greatest legacy we can leave our kids is to be a good example."

Dr. Vader started filling the gap about nine years ago when a social worker went to a child's house to find out why the child wasn't getting physical therapy. The reason was that the child had to have orthopedic shoes to go forward with therapy and the family couldn't afford them. Medicaid paid for therapy but not for orthopedics. When Dr. Vader found out, she gave $200 out of her own pocket for the shoes. After that it was $100 here, $100 there, until she had spent nearly $30,000 from her own pocket to provide for those in need. This was when she decided to start a foundation.

Looking for an established partner, she went first to the Department of Health and Human Services. "They have a thirty-day waiting period for help," she learned. "These people don't have thirty days. The whole point was to provide quick assistance for basic needs." The Community Foundation in Montrose was a better fit. Mary now heads the Helping Hand Fund under the Community Foundation umbrella. When a child needs shoes or reading glasses, or a family needs rent for a month or two, Helping Hand is there to fill the gap.

They might buy a car battery so a father can get to his job. Another grant was for a new transformer for a home ventilator. They keep a stock of gas cards so families can drive to medical appointments in other cities. "It has been fun to watch the fund grow and to give back to the neighborhood," she said. "This has been a dream of mine for a long time."

One of the foundation board's favorite projects was remodeling a bathroom for a dwarf child, who would likely grow up to be only three feet tall. My mom, who also serves on Mary's board, said they had countless discussions on how to help the family and how the bathroom was truly needed. The foundation did all the demo work with volunteers, then installed a pint-sized vanity and toilet, all for $2,000—in pink, no less!

The foundation is committed to helping recipients be self-supporting and independent. "When we buy a car battery, for example," Dr. Vader says, "we've not only given someone a lift, we've also empowered them to help themselves and maybe someone else. I think empowering someone might be more help than the actual money. We have found that help is best found through networking and relationships. Most of our requests come from people who know the recipient (social worker, minister, teachers) and they have established a relationship and can gauge how well the recipient will do."

Helping Hand Fund is committed to being a hand up, not a handout. Requests from a third-party referral bring the best results. Requests from the people themselves are the least reliable, and they're most likely to ask for repeated assistance. "We make it clear that this is a one-time grant," Mary explains. "They need to figure out how to move forward. Often, our board will vote to pay half or part of the request and give the applicant ideas of where else to go."

Like many successful nonprofits, Helping Hand encourages its recipients to pay it forward to help others as the foundation has helped them. The most powerful example of that is a story that still brings tears to my mother's eyes.

Summer 2013 was starting out like any other summer in Montrose. The snowmelt from the mountains comes rushing into our rivers, streams, reservoirs, and lakes. Sometimes the outdoor temperature climbs into the triple digits. That's when a day picnicking and swimming makes for a great family outing.

On this particular summer day some seventeen-year-old boys went swimming in the local pond. One Latino boy didn't know how to swim and he drowned. Several of his friends tried to save him but couldn't get to him in time. Though his parents were hard workers, they were undocumented. There was no way they could pay for a funeral. "It was a devastating tragedy for the community. It tore the town apart," Mary remembers. She and her board had an emergency meeting and went to the local funeral home for help. The funeral home agreed to pay for everything except the casket and the grave. Helping Hand paid the rest. All they asked in return was that the boy's family and friends pay it forward.

Less than two months later, the boy's friends, who had been with him the night he died, started a scholarship drive to give free swim lessons to those who couldn't afford it. The one who came up with the idea had also been a Helping Hand recipient. Very quickly the boys had more than twenty scholarships! That Helping Hand grant for funeral expenses gave these grieving kids a purpose and a way to honor their fallen friend. They also probably saved some lives. And they paid it forward by filling a gap in their own community in a meaningful, powerful way.

Teaching and Healing

Children who have continuous medical needs miss so much school that a typical education program does not work for them. This doesn't mean they are not smart. They have just missed a ton of school and they need help both medically and educationally. The average student who enters the kindergarten through eighth grade school at National Jewish Health comes in two to three years behind where he or she should be. When we learned about this remarkable school we immediately wanted to get involved. Our foundation did not have a lot of experience giving to medical needs, but we did understand education.

The school is housed on the National Jewish Health campus in Denver, which was cofounded in the early 1900s by Frances Wisebart Jacobs (who also helped start United Way) as a free hospital for homeless patients suffering from tuberculosis. The school serves ninety to one hundred students. Some of the kids live almost 30 miles away and take up to three public buses to get to and from school. Being accepted to this school is a privilege beyond belief. Every morning, a nurse checks their vitals, administers the proper medicines, and makes sure they get a healthy breakfast before their first class greets each student. By the eighth grade, students have learned to manage their own medicines, are learning and performing at grade level, and are ready to enter high school. Many of these students are accepted to Denver's top charter and private schools.

Education isn't the only gap that National Jewish Health fills. Since its inception, not one patient has been turned away for lack of ability to pay. In fact, it was a free hospital for the first seventy years of its existence. Early on, when people from around the country had asthma or other respiratory diseases, they went to National Jewish Health. Their tuberculosis treatment was known throughout the country for being the best. The hospital walls are adorned with photos showing the history of the patients and the history of the treatments.

As we got to know CEO Michael Salem (this is the same Michael Salem who went hiking with David Wick and me) it was clear that we could do more than help fill the education gap at the school. Michael taught us about the gap in Colorado health care. National Jewish Health was bursting at the seams and needed a new hospital. The new hospital and outpatient clinics would serve patients from all over the world with leading-edge treatment for asthma, allergies, eczema, lung diseases, and other specialties. National Jewish Health had created the most impressive fellowship training programs in the world. The new hospital would allow these programs and treatments to expand.

After years of getting to know each other and learning about the complexities of the medical field, my husband and I made our first ever mega gift to a hospital. As an honor to us, they recently renamed the school Morgridge Academy. This school is what is known as a facility school. A facility school is an alternative educational option designed to deliver quality education to students in residential treatment facilities, hospitals, and other non-traditional settings. National Jewish Health's medical campus is unique, because it hosts one of the only facility schools in the country that rotates medical faculty through the hallways, impacting the health and wellness of the students on a daily basis. Yet, if you ever get the privilege to visit the school and meet the kids, the experience is similar to every other high-performing school we've seen.

Another special feature of National Jewish Health and the school is the research and clinical support of Academic Fellows. We met the first cohort of Morgridge Fellows (medical students in the process of earning their residency), who are finishing fellowship training in medical research and clinical specialties and will soon be on their way to amazing medical careers throughout the United States. Michael said that our gift to National Jewish Health transformed how they looked at the school and at the fellows program. With medical care in the United States facing an uncertain future, I am confident that National Jewish Health will continue to fill the gaps in patient care and medical research, because they Never say Never™ to a patient in need.

Two young Morgridge Academy scholars learning and exploring on their campus at National Jewish Health.

New Opportunities

Madison, Wisconsin, is near and dear to our hearts. Not only is our daughter attending undergraduate school there but also both of John's parents are graduates of the University of Wisconsin. John and Tashia are known throughout the state for their amazing generosity. A program I want to highlight is the program they created called the Fund For Wisconsin Scholars. The Wisconsin Scholars allows any student who qualifies for Pell Grants— which are federally funded tuition grants—to receive additional support to get through college. Thousands of students have now benefited from this generosity, giving them more access to high-quality education.

Our challenge was to give in the Madison community without duplicating the efforts of John and Tashia. After two years of research and study, the gap we decided to fill was a workforce-training program. We found a great partnership through the YWCA. They had an empty space that was in need of a transformative gift to become a training classroom. This classroom quickly became filled with desks, teaching spaces, and ample technology to serve their clients. We also helped with the funding of a director for the first year of this program. Since we donated the initial seed money, the YWCA has gone on to become self-sustaining by winning grants from the state's Department of Workforce Development and is now called the YWeb Career Academy.

So far this year, they have completed two training courses with a total of twenty-six graduates. Of these, seventeen are minorities and four are women. Thirteen currently have family-wage-paying jobs, and the remaining graduates are working with the staff to seek employment.

This grant became one of my favorites because it filled a gap in a completely different sector other than education. (For us, this was out of our comfort zone and way outside our usual funding box.) We had to reset our questions to the nonprofit because we had never given to a job creation program before. The outcome is huge for the lives of the people who worked hard to graduate from the Career Academy and become self-sustaining citizens by getting a hand up, not a handout. I never thought we would be assisting to train people for careers at the YWCA, but that's where we saw a gap we could fill. I couldn't be more proud of their work and the lives they are rebuilding!

A Simple Wish

Recently I got a fresh reminder that a gift doesn't have to be big to make a big impact. Each year Colorado boasts about its Bike to Work Day and Bike to School Day. These special events promote so many things from health and wellness to environmental concerns to self-sufficiency. At one of the schools my friend Kellie Lauth oversees, they fully promoted Bike to School day and learned a very disturbing lesson: out of nine hundred students, only four showed up with a bike. Thirty more wanted to participate, but they had no bikes.

My associate John Farnam found out about this and immediately made some calls that led to a meeting with Wish for Wheels, a nonprofit foundation whose mission is to give as many kids as possible brand new bikes and helmets. It brings communities together, gives many of us the opportunity to give back, and most important puts a whole lot of smiles on a whole lot of faces. According to the Wish for Wheels website (www.wishforwheels .org), one in five children in the Denver Metro area lives in poverty and for them a bike is a mere dream.

The school, our foundation, and Wish for Wheels came up with a plan that volunteer teachers would build the bikes at the beginning of the school year. Then, the school received a grant to purchase every second grader in the school a bike. This was a three-part win. The nonprofit Wish for Wheels serves its mission, the teachers bond while building sixty bikes, and last and most important the students are going to be surprised and excited to receive a bike from their teacher who built it for them. Their principal is working on other programs to take this to the next level in physical education and health classes, so the grant keeps giving.

In the great scheme of things this is a small program, not something that deals with life-or-death issues. But it does so much in promoting safety, in giving students not only transportation but also pride of ownership, and in providing a new way for teachers to invest in their students. It's something you could do in your own neighborhood. The bikes we bought cost $100 each, well within the reach of most donors. This is the kind of project where a little investment brings a lot of joy.

Principal Kellie Lauth of STEM Launch surprising her second grade students with free, brand new bikes and helmets provided through Wish for Wheels.

Chapter 13

Making an Impact

John and I are often referred to as venture philanthropists. We are always looking for new and innovative ways to solve existing or undiscovered challenges in our community. To fully embody this philosophy we must be keen observers, excellent listeners, and notice nuances or unique opportunities and move quickly on them. We believe in sharing what we learn, especially from the people and programs that truly captivate us and make a significant positive impact on others.

It is fair to say I notice everything. Sometimes this is a distraction, and sometimes it leads to unexpected adventures. During an annual KIPP Summer Summit in Las Vegas, I attended a lunch with New Jersey Governor Chris Christie. As I was leaving the room after the event I noticed a woman in the most incredible shoes I've ever seen. They were gold colored, and the heels looked like stacks of ribbon. You had to see them to believe them. I immediately introduced myself to this woman. Her name is Mandy Williams—a retired business executive. I learned that along with her sister, Tina Pennington—a stay-at-home mom, she had written a book titled *What I Learned About Life When My Husband Got Fired!* Tina's nickname is Red and Mandy's nickname is Black. Red and Black had written their book as an idea for a sitcom but soon after, it was launched by Neiman Marcus, the famous Texas-based department store. This started new careers for the two of them as experts on financial literacy. Since they had been teaching in the KIPP Houston high school, they'd been invited to the KIPP Summer Summit.

Although financial literacy isn't exactly a part of STEM education—science, technology, engineering, and mathematics— the idea of teaching it to high school students is a stroke of genius (and balancing a checkbook does require math skills). What good does it do to teach children the skills they need to make money unless we also teach them how to manage it? Clearly Red and Black had to share their knowledge with our teachers at Share Fair Nation. These women are outliers— they're so far out of the box, they rock!

We invited Red and Black to travel with Share Fair Nation and share their story. We were willing to see if the teachers at a technology conference would have any interest in teaching their own students about financial literacy in a fun and engaging way. The ladies' first appearance with us was at the University of Central Florida. As teachers heard about their program, they started ditching the seminars they'd signed up for to hear these two instead. Teachers were not only begging to bring these innovative financial management concepts into their classrooms, they were also using them in managing their own personal budgets. I adopted some of their advice myself, and now I save money every year on stuff I don't even miss.

I couldn't keep these two crazy-wonderful women to myself; I had to share them. Black really wowed me when I recommended her to Dave Krepcho of Second Harvest Food Bank of Orlando. My hope was that the connection would continue the circle of teaching and learning we'd seen in that great organization. I'm glad to report the result was a home run. Dave immediately saw the impact this teaching could have on his organization, his partners, and his clients.

Red and Black started out helping KIPP, one of our grant recipients, and have now come full circle to be our expert consultants on financial literacy. We recommend them to a lot of organizations. The people we introduce them to see that they have developed a fun way to explain finances and other Life 101 topics by using their own life experiences. One of the education obstacles they face, that we have a lot of experience in, is that a school has to get school board approval to teach financial literacy. I helped them jump over that hurdle by starting a book club. If there are bureaucratic roadblocks between you and a brilliant teaching idea, go the entrepreneurial route. Learn to steer around the system without breaking the rules and rubbing administrators the wrong way. Chances are you'll need their help later on.

While I've come to depend on Black (Mandy), she kindly gives me credit for helping push through the educational bureaucracy. "When I say something, I'm either a 'textbook salesman' or that crazy woman from Texas," she told me. "When my audience knows you and I are on the same wavelength, it provides validation; not to mention support and knowing we're not alone." Like so many good and trusted programs our foundation is investing in, Red and Black's program can start very modestly, with one $25 book. And yes, their book is life changing!

From a quiet start in the education world at KIPP Houston to my introduction to Second Harvest Food Bank of Central Florida in Orlando—Red and Black have carried their financial literacy program nationwide. This includes prisons, where inmates said that if they'd had this teaching on the outside they might not be in prison today. Schools are now using videos of these inmates to start conversations about the importance of financial literacy. And the circle of sharing continues.

As I have mentioned several times, once we find superstar leaders like Red and Black who have an impressive program that works—the first thing we do is introduce them to many of our colleagues, or what we like to say, dot connecting. We introduced Red and Black's book to Tyler, our Madison colleague, and he has brought their book to the men he is working with in the corrections system.

Tyler said, "We have been given approval for the men to have the books in the jail. The group met for an hour today. We had a robust conversation about the language of finance and how it can be used to oppress. We continue to bring the conversation back to the idea that knowledge is power.

"The group has had many unforeseen positive outcomes. One is that the book club approach created an opportunity for resource networking. The financial literacy program opened a door that led to an effective peer referral system. Today one of the younger inmates asked me for additional business cards to share with his peers that are not allowed to leave the jail. He wanted to make sure they could contact me after their release.

"Many good things are happening . . . an inmate released last week asked me for some housing resources before he left. He returned today to thank me for a suggestion I made and for encouraging him to keep his job. He identified that sticking out the job opened the door for the transitional housing I suggested.

"The men quickly identified that it may be difficult for them to relate to the book because it is ethnocentric, having a white middle-class perspective. I explained, 'We can criticize the perspective, but can also value and learn from the information.' They liked that, they want to be able to question and comment on some of the things Red took for granted or the life experiences that were foreign to their lives. The makeup of the group is about 85 percent African-American, 13 percent White, 1 percent Asian, and 1 percent Latino.

"The book club process has demonstrated to the inmates how to effectively communicate as a group and to advocate as a collective. Many of the men were empowered to share their financial expertise. For example, one man shared that he has been in the car sales business for more than twenty-five years and spoke about the 'true' cost of owning a vehicle. He laid out the pros and cons of taking out a note on a car purchase. The discussion about finances raised some interesting topics, such as child support and what it means to be a contributing father (emotionally, physically, spiritually, economically, etc.). I can say that my professional experience has taught me the power of recognizing the positives in an otherwise frustrating situation."

Returning a Favor

A few summers ago we were hanging with my in-laws in New Hampshire. Tashia brought me an article that she had saved from *San Jose Mercury News* about an organization she had been supporting for teachers called Resource Area For Teachers (RAFT). Mary Simon founded RAFT in San Jose. Mary would go to manufacturers in Silicon Valley and ask for their leftover scraps to use as resources for teachers. With those raw materials, Mary worked with all kinds of teachers, scientists, and inventors to create hands-on science and math learning kits for kids. RAFT then attached an instructional sheet for other teachers to use. There are now over seven hundred free idea sheets available online for any teacher anywhere in the world. All math and science kits are aligned to Common Core State Standards curricula. And RAFT has what they call a green room, a workspace just for teachers to access equipment and advice to create new kits.

Tashia explained to my husband and me that RAFT might be worth expanding to Colorado because the model worked really well and the teachers loved RAFT. It's also great for the environment, which is a big issue in Colorado. Over 95 percent of all RAFT kits are made from discarded materials that might have been thrown in the dump. They are now turned into teaching tools.

Within months we had hired a top-notch executive director for the state, Stephanie Welsh, and asked her to introduce the RAFT nonprofit business and concept to Denver. Since then, RAFT has gained thousands of teacher members and has saved millions of pounds of materials from going into the landfill. But Stephanie isn't stopping there. I can tell you she has national aspirations!

Since my in-laws had shared a great success with me, I wanted to return the favor. The next summer John and I told them about the impact we were having with Book Trust. We explained how easy it was to get started, the immediate impact it was having, and most important how they absolutely had to attend a book day delivery and see how excited the students were when the teacher opened that big box and handed out the new books the kids had been waiting for. With their deep passion for literacy, the senior Morgridges have sponsored Book Trust in the schools they support in both California and Wisconsin. We try as a family not to replicate grants because there is so much need in so many places. We each follow our own passions and preferences in giving. But as a part of that, we share our successes and encourage other family members to try things in their world that have worked well in ours.

Sharing the success you find in people and organizations that make an impact seems extremely obvious. Yet sometimes we get so focused on the moment and we don't realize that the idea we're developing in one place could do wonders somewhere else; or that another school, or neighborhood, or nonprofit could learn from our experience. Be sure to recognize the major impact your investments and the people you support are making and share your success with others. Don't be shy about asking what works elsewhere that you could put to work in your own area. They might not all be as gonzo fun as Red and Black, or as innovative as John and Tashia, but a good idea is a good idea no matter where you put it.

Chapter 14

Take the First Step

othing makes me happier and gives me more fulfillment than knowing I've been able to give someone a hand up—to throw one more starfish back into the sea. Giving with passion is easy and exciting. Turning your passion into impact requires homework, research, consultation with friends and experts, and a careful look at the numbers. It also means an occasional sleepless night, dumb mistakes, and tears of both joy and frustration. It's hard work, but I enjoy it more than anything in the world.

As I was talking to a friend about writing this book, he asked, "Why do you go to so much trouble to give your money away? Why do you give it away at all? Why not buy an island and spend your days in a hammock drinking something cold out of a tall glass with a little paper umbrella?"

Fair question.

The answer is that in spite of all the money and success in my life, I'm still Carrie. Still the grocery store checker who was so thrilled with her first $100-a-month apartment. Still the ambitious real estate office worker who dreamed of running her own business. Still the sleep-deprived cocktail waitress who promised herself a better future even if she wasn't sure how she'd get there.

I am the starfish.

I'm the low-income, high-potential kid I've seen on my site visits to schools over the years. I'm the one who has made mistakes, taken some wrong turns, and needed a hand up once in a while. I'm the one who was rescued time and again by a loving parent, a dedicated teacher, a bible study teacher, a compassionate boss, or someone else who believed in me, encouraged me, and gave me a chance when I needed it.

Most of all, my husband John has encouraged, supported, and guided me in refining my philosophy of giving and in everything else in my life. We make a perfect team on the foundation: I'm the accelerator and he's the brake. I'm all about moving ahead while John tends to take the broader, more deliberate view. Through him and through my own life experience, I've come to believe that success and opportunity carry responsibility. I got help when I needed it. I think it's only right, now that I have the means, to pay it forward by helping others.

I work tirelessly for people I'll never meet because I know there are untold numbers of starfish out there who need my support and involvement. But as I've said before, the need always outruns the available resources.

That's where you come in.

Remember that for every dollar that comes from a big donor, the average American household gives $5. Big gifts get the media's attention, but at the end of the day, your donations of money, time, love, encouragement, and other support go further and do more. You have the power to change the path of someone's life. How you choose to spend your donation dollars makes a difference.

So donate to a project or a program you believe in. Maybe it's schools and education like I support. Maybe it's abused children, or animals, or your church, or a social cause. Your passion for the work is just as important as the financial gift. If you fritter away your giving budget on charities that are merely convenient or persistent, you've lost an opportunity to follow your true passion. If giving produces that warm, satisfying feeling that tells you you've done something worthwhile, you know your money's in the right place. It comes down to a combination of giving with the head and with the heart. You want causes that spend your money wisely and make every dollar work hard for them the way you worked hard to earn it.

There's also that need to help others that sings to your heart. Whether you're giving $5 or a lot more, the goal should be the same. The feeling you get from knowing $5 has been well used is the same feeling we get at the foundation when we realize our goal has been met. There is a beautiful Bible verse from 2 Corinthians 9:7 that I love, "Each of you should give what you have decided in your heart to give, not reluctantly or under compulsion, for God loves a cheerful giver." That joy and love of sharing what we have connects all givers everywhere.

In telling my story I've talked about a lot of other people. To me giving is definitely a group activity. I look to others to tell me what a prospective grantee is like, to tell me what they need, to spend the money wisely, and to share the joy and burden of getting the job done. Though we live in a technologically advanced world, joining hands as human beings is still the only way to move forward. Some of my most rewarding friendships are with people I met in the process of researching or making a gift. The staff and supporters of nonprofits are great places to meet new friends. You already share a common interest with them, and working together will strengthen the bond between you. Maybe you sit on a committee together, or volunteer on the same day. All these things take you out of yourself and make you part of a team.

It's teams, not individuals, that make real progress in the world of philanthropy. As many gifts as John and I have given over the years, I can't think of a single project where we donated the entire cost. Except in rare cases, I don't believe in being a single-source donor. When you share the responsibility, you also share in the joy and satisfaction of reaching the goal. No one donor can do it all. There's no such thing as a stand-alone philanthropist. But your gift and mine, together with many others, can work miracles.

Inspired givers share a passion for their cause and a willingness to work with others. They also share an attitude of optimism, persistence, and hope for the future. As careful as I am in researching my gifts, I've made some big mistakes. I've misread people, been blindsided by nonprofits that weren't what they seemed, and cried over lost resources, wasted time, and squandered opportunities. If you reach out to help others, I promise you will make mistakes. Don't be afraid to fail. As in life, if an opportunity doesn't work out, pivot and try again. Admit your mistakes, learn from them, and go on. This will only make you stronger, wiser, and more grateful for success down the line.

Whatever resources and abilities you're born with, whatever the world throws your way, attitude is the one variable you can control. I found attitude to be the underlying key to the success of our foundation and to the grantees we invest in. Those who have a can-do attitude end up being our favorite grantees. Whatever obstacles they face, they figure out a way to get around them and move forward.

Attitude is important not only in pursuing goals but also in dealing with people. People who work at nonprofits are too often overqualified and underpaid but believe so strongly in their cause that they dedicate their careers to it. Be nice to them and be open to learning from their experience. There's a tendency in the business world to assume nonprofits should pay their people less than in the for-profit world. I often hear of talented, dedicated people taking huge pay cuts to work for a nonprofit. This is exactly backward and should change immediately. Nonprofit workers and executives have as much responsibility and need as many skills as anybody else. They should be recruited at the same level as a profitable public or private company and earn competitive salaries.

Attitude also means focusing on the positive. Tony Hsieh, CEO of the incredibly successful online shoe store Zappos.com, wrote an entire book, *Delivering Happiness: A Path to Profits, Passion, and Purpose* (New York: Business Plus, 2010), about positive culture in the work environment. Among other inspirations, this book made me realize that I used to spend 80 percent of my time talking about what was broken in the causes I supported. After one of my grants failed in a large public school, I found myself depressed and crying. The students weren't going to get the health care that they needed and the politics had become so toxic they crowded out the positive thoughts and good work that was created.

I took a big step back after that day. To be honest, I was broken down and ready to give up. That's when I decided to hit the reset button. Giving should be fun. You should feel joy and a huge sense of satisfaction when you give. I had gotten too far into the trees to see the forest. I decided at that moment that our foundation would no longer fight to give away money. This doesn't mean we don't stand up for what is right, but we no longer fight. The culture in an organization is now crucial to our giving. We don't hesitate to pull out of a grant or an event if the culture is toxic. The result is that I now spend 80 percent of my time talking about what *is* working. I let the other stuff go. We still face tough issues dealing with poverty, homelessness, foster care, and more, but we do it with a new attitude of what can work and what is possible.

The fun part about giving is looking ahead. I sometimes ask myself how my philanthropy will change in the future. The fact is I have no idea. The future hasn't been invented yet and so I don't know where my passion for giving will lead me. What I *can* do, and what John and I do every year, is hold back 10 percent of our annual giving budget for unexpected opportunities. When we make our budget at the beginning of the fiscal year we have some idea of what we want to do, but we know there will be surprises. The 10 percent for the future gives us a chance to make a difference in ways we couldn't even think of.

In a way, all giving is an investment that says you have hope for the future, that what you do today will make a difference tomorrow. Right now you may be able to reach out to others, or you may be one of those many starfish who needs a hand up. I hope that if you give, it will be out of gratitude for what you have and a desire to enjoy that sense of satisfaction you won't get any other way. If you are in need, I hope you will accept help with a humble heart and that you'll express your thanks to the people responsible.

It's a full circle: giving and receiving, teaching and learning, paying it forward. Best of all, it's a circle that keeps moving and growing. Most of the stories I've written about aren't finished yet. And there are many more that I didn't mention (maybe I'll put them in another book!). All I can do is give you a snapshot of the action that I hope will convey some of the energy and excitement and potential ahead as the circle continues. Someone out there today is the Sal Khan or Hadi Partovi of tomorrow. My young friend Kylan is back from Africa and oh what a story he has to tell. Together you and I can find and fund the Kylans of the world who will grow up to shape our future.

Whoever we are, whatever we have, the act of giving ties us together. I encourage you to take the first step toward the joy of giving by listening to your heart, hearing what's important, and connecting with others who share your vision. You and I can lift each other up by sharing the gifts the world has given us. Together we can join hands and take on whatever challenge the future has in store. Whether our contribution is a little or a lot, together—and only together—we can make the world a better place, one gift at a time.

Because every gift matters.

Acknowledgments

I want to say thank you to John and Tashia Morgridge for giving both John and me the most incredible opportunity . . . the gift of giving back.

To my husband, for over twenty years he has looked lovingly at me and has encouraged me to live my dream.

To my team, John, Sarah, and Kim, we can't live without you!

Appendix

GIVING CHECKLIST

- Have you ever identified your giving passion?

- Have you ever given to that cause?

- If the outcome was good, did you tell your friends about it and network more people to get involved and help too?

- Have you had a successful gift?

- If so, could you compare this gift to others you are considering?

- Was it a gift of money, of time, of talent?

- If the outcome was negative, would you work with the group/organization to fix it or just move on?

- If you got involved with the organization in other areas besides giving a gift, would the organization flourish with your leadership, insight, and skills, or do you prefer to write a check for support?

- What type of support do you want to give?
  - Checks
  - Volunteering
  - Mentorship
  - Advising
  - Board service
  - Marketing
  - Strategic planning
  - Start a new program with them, with you guiding it
  - Are you a matching donor, or does your money require a match?

- Where do you think you can have the most impact?

- How many people will be affected by your gift? Are you okay with that number?

- Have you looked at their work or checked out their website?

- Do you know someone in the organization that you can have an honest conversation with?

- What do you expect to get out of the gift?

- What do they expect to get out of your gift?
  - Are they the same goals?

- What is your expectation of time?

- Do they have to spend your money immediately or is this a long-term project?

While writing this book, I have to admit, I kept asking myself to be on the lookout for "IT." Well I found it. The surprise to me was that it wasn't a thing; it was passion. I met teachers this year at Share Fair Nation who were so full of passion they were bursting at the seams. What I was looking for had been in front of me and with me the entire time. I just had to see and experience it to realize that I had found it!

Notes

1. National Philanthropic Trust, Resources for Donors, "Charitable Giving Statistics," http://www.nptrust.org/philanthropic-resources/charitable -giving-statistics/.
2. Giving USA: The Annual Report on Philanthropy, a publication of Giving USA Foundation,™ researched and written by the Indiana University Lilly Family School of Philanthropy.
3. National Philanthropic Trust, Resources for Donors, "Charitable Giving Statistics," http://www.nptrust.org/philanthropic-resources/charitable -giving-statistics/.
4. "Interview with Amy Friedman," Repaving Main Street with Bill Cobb, KRCN radio show, February 21, 2013, http://www.booktrust.org/sites /default/files/Media/KRCN_Amy%20Friedman%20Interview.mp3.
5. The Annie E. Casey Foundation, "Education," http://www.aecf.org/work /education/; Sarah D. Sparks, "Study: Third Grade Reading Predicts Later High School Graduation," Education Week Blog, April 8, 2011, http://blogs .edweek.org/edweek/inside-school-research/2011/04/the_disquieting_side _effect_of.html.
6. "Ironman Triathlon," Wikipedia, last modified October 15, 2014, http:// en.wikipedia.org/wiki/Ironman_Triathlon.
7. GuideStar, "About Us: Why Should You Care about Nonprofit Information," http://www.guidestar.org/rxg/about-us/index.aspx.
8. "Disruptive Innovation," Clayton Christensen Institute, http://www .christenseninstitute.org/key-concepts/disruptive-innovation-2/?gclid=Cj0K EQjwn4iiBRDFh76wlfCVuYABEiQAwWJ1IsbXMUCx8XIQm02awFCEcw6I p0bGCz-eRXCkK-5WKzkaAmA78P8HAQ.

9. Johns Hopkins University, Center for Civil Society Studies, "Announcing the 3rd Edition of America's Nonprofit Sector: A Primer," June 28, 2012, http://ccss.jhu.edu/announcing-the-3rd-edition-of-americas-nonprofit-sector-a-primer.

10. GuideStar, "About Us: Why Should You Care about Nonprofit Information," http://www.guidestar.org/rxg/about-us/index.aspx.

11. Roots and Shoots, "Although Small in Stature First Graders, Inspired by Jane Goodall, Do BIG People Work," submitted June 23, 2014, http://www.rootsandshoots.org/content/although-small-stature-first-graders-empowered-jane-goodall-do-big-people-work.

12. Tennyson Center for Children, "Our Children's Stories: Andrea," http://www.tennysoncenter.org/page.aspx?pid=279.

13. Jamie Van Leeuwen biography, Yatedo, http://www.yatedo.com/p/Jamie+Van+Leeuwen/normal/1f9da5815d906bfc396660fdeefd8713.

14. Metro Denver Homeless Initiative, "2013 Homeless Point-in-Time Study," www.denversroadhome.org/files/2013-Denver-Metro-Point-in-Time.pdf.

15. Robert Goodman, "Opening Access to STEM Careers," https://njctl.org/_/wp.../public-Opening-Access-to-STEM-Careers_.pdf.

16. Wendy Chiado, "Predicting High School Completion Using Student Performance in High School Algebra," PhD diss., University of Colorado at Denver, 2012.

17. Florida Department of Children and Families.

18. Ibid.

19. James H. Fowler and Nicholas A. Christakis, "Cooperative Behavior Cascades in Human Social Networks," PNAS 107(12), March 23, 2010, 5334–5338.

20. Colorado Department of Human Services, "Average Daily Out-of-Home Population per 1000," https://rom.socwel.ku.edu/CO_Public/AllViews.aspx?RVID=636.

21. Colorado Department of Human Services, "Time in Care for Children Emancipating from Placement," https://rom.socwel.ku.edu/CO_Public/AllViews.aspx?RVID=42.

22. United Way of the Columbia–Willamette, "Dreamer and Doer: Frances Wisebart Jacobs, 'Mother of Charities,'" March 5, 2013, http://uwpdx.blogspot.com/2013/03/dreamer-and-doer-frances-wisebart.html.

23. Hadi and Ali Partovi, "What 90% of Schools Don't Teach," Huffington Post, updated April 28, 2013, http://www.huffingtonpost.com/hadi-and-ali-partovi/teach-coding-schools_b_2759066.html.

24. "About Jane Goodall's Roots and Shoots," http://www.janegoodall.org/programs/rootsandshoots/about.

About the Author

Carrie Morgridge currently serves as the Morgridge Family Foundation's vice president. Over the past few years, Carrie and her husband, John, have defined the philanthropic focus of the foundation on transformative gifts in education, conservation, the arts, and health and wellness.

The foundation has been instrumental in supporting major capital projects at the Denver Museum of Nature and Science, National Jewish Health, University of Central Florida, University of Denver, Mile High United Way, KIPP Schools, The Nature Conservancy, and Second Harvest Food Bank of Orlando, Florida.

Carrie founded Student Support Foundation, a youth philanthropy club, to cultivate high school and college philanthropists and teach them the importance of giving through hands-on learning.

Carrie Morgridge was an integral part of the team that created Share Fair Nation. This national event has trained thousands of teachers on how to integrate technology in the classroom, and promotes inquiry-based learning coupled with creativity. STEMosphere, the public side to Share Fair Nation, has allowed students, teachers, and families to experience hands-on/brains-on learning and fun. STEMosphere allows the students to learn side by side with the teachers who attend the event. Thus far, the Share Fair Nation event has provided 300,000 hours of FREE high-quality professional development for teachers.

In 2010, Carrie Morgridge received the distinguished Frances Wisebart Jacobs award from Mile High United Way. She currently serves on the Board of Trustees at the University of Denver, the Denver Museum of Nature and Science, Colorado Mountain College Board of Overseers, and New Jersey Center for Teaching and Learning. She has been publicly recognized for her work at National Jewish Hospital and Denver Academy. Carrie serves in an advisory capacity and speaks nationally to education advocacy and technology-focused forums.

Carrie and her husband divide their time between Colorado and Florida. She graduated summa cum laude from the International Academy of Design and Technology. She is an avid outdoorsman and has competed in nine Ironman Competitions, several marathons, Muddy Buddy, and Warrior Dash.